DUDLEY PUBLIC LIBRARIES

The loan of this book may be renewed if not required by other readers, by contacting the library from which it was borrowed.

Published by
British Association for Adoption & Fostering
(BAAF)
Skyline House
200 Union Street
London SE1 0LX
www.baaf.org.uk

Charity registration 275689

British Library Cataloguing in Publication Data
A catalogue reference record for this book is available from the
British Library

ISBN 1 903699 24 X

All photographs posed by models
by Digital Vision and John Birdsall
www.johnbirdsall.co.uk
Project management by Jo Francis, BAAF
Designed by Andrew Haig & Associates
Typeset by Avon DataSet Ltd, Bidford on Avon, Warwickshire
Printed by Creative Print and Design

BAAF Adoption & Fostering is the leading UK-wide membership
organisation for all those concerned with adoption, fostering and
child care issues.

Contents

Acknowledgements

I would like to acknowledge the incredible generosity of the many foster carers who have shared their experiences with me, during the 14 years I've been involved in fostering issues. I never cease to be amazed at how willing foster carers – who are some of the busiest, most time-stretched people I know – are to give their valuable time to passing on thoughts and insights they hope will be helpful to other carers, and to the children and young people they care for. There are some truly wonderful carers out there, and they continue to be an enormous inspiration to me.

And I'd equally like to thank all the children and young people in foster care whom I've met or talked to over the years. Again, their generosity in sharing their personal views and experiences with me has been incredible. Their resilience, their determination and their desire to help other children in similar situations continue to amaze me. And I can't pass by an opportunity to say a very personal thank you to my good friend, Benni-Jo Tyler – a very special and remarkable young woman – whose support and trust have opened so many doors for me.

I would also like to thank Jennifer Lord (BAAF), Jane Asquith (BAAF), Deborah Cullen (BAAF), Barbara Hudson (BAAF), Marjorie Morrison (BAAF) and Jane Gillespie (Croham Fostering) for reading the manuscript, and for their helpful comments.

Finally, I want to thank the social workers who have taken the time to help me develop my knowledge of adoption and fostering. So often they are the last to be recognised and the first to be blamed by those who understand so little of the complex and demanding work they do. But there are so many truly remarkable people around, who I've been privileged to work with in BAAF, in Fostering Network and in many adoption and fostering agencies around the country.

On a purely personal note, I'd like to dedicate this book to the memory of Rose Lang and Donna Beckles, two very special colleagues from BAAF, whose very sudden and unexpected deaths

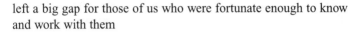

left a big gap for those of us who were fortunate enough to know and work with them

Henrietta Bond
July 2004

The quotations in this book

The quotations in this book have been taken from several sources:

Personal communication to the author

Foster Care magazine, issues 110, 113 and 115, published by Fostering Network

Fostering Attachments, by Brian Cairns, published by BAAF in 2004

Growing up in Foster Care, by Gillian Schofield, Mary Beek and Kay Sargent, published by BAAF in 2000

Not Just a Name: The views of young people in foster and residential care, by Barbara Fletcher, published by The Who Cares? Trust and the National Consumer Council in 1993

Part of the Family, by Gillian Schofield, published by BAAF in 2002

Testing the Limits of Foster Care, by Moira Walker, Malcolm Hill and John Triseliotis, published by BAAF in 2002

Note about the author

Henrietta Bond is a freelance journalist and media consultant, specialising in children and family issues. Her interest in looked after children began when she became BAAF's press officer in 1990, and since becoming freelance in 1995 she has worked with Fostering Network, The Who Cares? Trust, NCH, Barnardo's, TalkAdoption, A National Voice, and many other children and young people's organisations, and local authorities. She has written for *Guardian Society*, *Community Care*, *Care and Health*, *Children Now* and

Young People Now, and also recently authored a new edition of BAAF's Advice Note, *Fostering: Some questions answered.*

The Adolescent and Children's Trust (TACT)

BAAF is grateful to TACT for their generous financial support towards the production of this book.

TACT is a children's charity formed in 1993 whose mission is 'to help children of all ages and all ethnic groups to grow and develop as unique individuals through the continued creative development of appropriate child-centred services.'

Since that time, TACT has developed into a national organisation with six service units across England and Wales.

Services include task-centred fostering, parent and baby placements, permanency and adoption and outreach support.

TACT aims to recruit a diverse range of foster carers and develop their skills and expertise through comprehensive training and NVQ programmes. Regular support (including 24-hour telephone support) and supervision are provided by qualified supervising social workers.

TACT values its staff and foster carers and recognises their contribution to the delivery of the high standard of service for which TACT is well known.

TACT always seeks to internally review its practice and compare its performance with similar organisations. It encourages sharing good practice both on national and international fronts and consequently hosted a national workshop with BAAF, provided hospitality to social work visitors from Hong Kong and is looking to strengthen links with Ghana.

TACT remains committed to enhancing the services to the children for whom it cares whilst maximising their life chances. More information is available by calling 0800 085 3864 or visiting www.tactfostercare.org.uk.

Introduction

First it was wonderful, we could do whatever we wanted. But after a while we realised that we missed having children around. When we saw an advert for foster carers in the local paper, we responded.
Foster carers in *Foster Care*, issue 113

Have you ever wanted to do something which really makes a difference? Something which means that a child or young person who has no hope for the future can regain their confidence that the world is full of possibilities for discovery, achievement and happiness? It certainly won't happen overnight, and it'll probably take a lot of patience, perseverance and "stickability", but being a foster carer can offer you a unique opportunity to create brighter futures for children whose lives have become difficult and distressing.

Fostering is a way of providing a family life for children who cannot live with their own parents. It can be a very temporary arrangement, or one which lasts for several months or years, or for large parts of their childhood. Some children enter and leave foster care several times over a year. This makes it very hard to know exactly how many children and young people are fostered every year in the UK, but it's estimated that it's around 50,000.

There are many reasons why children and young people need foster care. It may be because their parent is ill, or unable to care for them for a while because of problems relating to drugs or alcohol. It may be because a child has been hurt, neglected or sexually abused by someone in, or living with, their family. Or it may be that there are lots of family tensions, and a young person and their family need a break from each other. In some cases the break is needed because the child has a physical or learning disability, and the family needs a short rest while the child enjoys new experiences in a new environment.

ǀ A shortage of carers

The UK charity Fostering Network estimates that there are about 37,000 foster carers in the UK, and that another 8,000 new carers are needed.

A shortage of foster carers doesn't always mean that children who need foster care won't be placed with a foster carer. But what it can mean is that a child is placed with the only foster carer who has a vacancy and is prepared to take them – rather than a foster carer who best matches the individual child's needs. For example, a teenager who would benefit from living with someone who is experienced in looking after teenagers and lives near to the young person's school and friends, ends up staying with a foster carer who lives on the other side of the region, who normally specialises in fostering younger children.

All sorts of people can become foster carers, because children and young people have such a wide range of needs. Some children will benefit from living in a two-parent household with lots of other children, but some may need the one-to-one attention of being the only child in the household, and may prefer living with only one adult. Fostering agencies welcome people who are single, married, divorced, co-habiting, gay or lesbian – as long as they are able to respond to the needs of children. Carers don't need to have their own children but they do need experience and understanding of caring for children, which might vary from babysitting for nephews and nieces to working as a teacher, social worker or sports coach.

And why do people become foster carers? There are as many reasons as there are different people caring for children and young people around the UK. Some people choose it because they enjoyed bringing up their own family and feel they still have lots to offer; some feel they have a wealth of professional or personal experience they can draw upon; and some say that they simply love having children in their lives. But when you ask foster carers what motivates them to continue through the times when the going gets tough, they'll tell you that it's the reward of knowing they have made a difference – however small – to the future of a child or young person.

| Fostering today

In the past, fostering was often seen as a way of putting a roof over a child's head, and that giving the child "love" was all that was needed. But today it is recognised that the important role of foster carers is to help children cope with difficult and painful experiences, regain their lost confidence, and prepare for the future. Therefore fostering agencies expect foster carers to work very closely with social workers, children's parents, and other professionals, in order to carry out an agreed plan for each child. Some foster carers choose to work as paid professionals whilst others retain the status of volunteers, but all carers receive a payment to cover the costs of having a child in their home.

Fostering agencies don't expect people to have all the skills needed to carry out the role of a foster carer. If they believe someone has the commitment, enthusiasm and child-centred attitude they are looking for, they offer preparation and training. All foster carers then have to be approved by a fostering panel in order to care for other people's children. Once they become foster carers they receive ongoing training and support so they can continue to develop these skills.

We believe that this book will answer many of your initial questions about fostering and help you understand more about this extremely important and demanding task. We have covered issues such as: how people become foster carers; what children feel about coming into care; how to settle a child into your home; the law and regulations; and working as part of the fostering team. Many of these issues are illustrated by the experiences of real foster carers, who speak openly about the things they've found difficult or challenging, as well as the rewards and high points of the task. And there are also quotes from young people who speak about their experiences of being in foster care and what they need from foster carers.

We are sure that from reading these quotes you will realise that fostering can make a big difference to the lives of unhappy, mixed-up children and young people. But restoring a child's faith in themselves and the world around them doesn't happen overnight, and is a demanding task. We hope this book will help you make a decision about whether this is something that you and your family (if you have one) are ready to consider.

| **Overview of the law**

Children who need fostering are in the care of local authorities – in other words, your local council. The local authority uses its own fostering team or the services of a voluntary or independent agency to find foster carers. The way that all fostering agencies operate is governed by law, guidance and regulations.

The main piece of legislation governing fostering in England and Wales is the Children Act 1989, and in Scotland it is the Children (Scotland) Act 1995. In England and Wales there are also National Minimum Standards for Fostering Services, and in Scotland there are National Care Standards for Foster Care and Family Placement Services.

In England and Wales some children needing foster placements will be looked after by their local authority under a court order made under the Children Act 1989. This allows the local authority to make decisions affecting the child and their child's future, even if the parents are not in agreement with this (although it's important to try and get the parents' agreement, wherever possible).

In Scotland, Children's Hearings make supervision requirements for children, where there are concerns or child protection issues. Supervision requirements may have conditions attached to them, for example, that the child lives with foster carers.

Parents can also ask that their children be looked after, because of problems in the family or because the parent is unwell and has no-one else to care for the child. This is a voluntary arrangement – often referred to as "accommodation". This is covered by the Children Act 1989 (England and Wales) and the Children (Scotland) Act 1995. Parents can take their children home whenever they wish – although wherever possible it's good to plan for a child to return home. In Scotland a parent has to give 14 days notice of their intention to do this, if the child has been accommodated for more than six months.

A child being cared for by a local authority used to be referred to as being "in care", but is now referred to as being "looked after".

Independent fostering provider (IFP)

This is the term used to describe independent agencies which recruit, train and support foster carers to look after children on behalf of local authorities (also known as independent fostering agencies (IFAs)). Local authorities approach IFPs when they do not have foster carers of their own who can meet the particular needs of a child. Independent fostering providers usually employ or pay fees to foster carers who work on their behalf, and they may also provide holiday pay and pensions. These agencies are required to meet the same standards as all other fostering agencies.

Court orders

A court may grant a variety of temporary, long-term or even permanent orders to safeguard the welfare of a child. For example, there are emergency protection orders and interim care orders designed to be used for few days or weeks while the child's and family's needs are assessed, and there are care orders which are made when plans for a child's future have been carefully considered, and which may last until a child is 18 years old. In Scotland, the court can make a parental responsibility order to the local authority which gives the authority parental rights regarding all decisions about a child except adoption.

| Scope of this edition

The contents of this book apply to England, Wales and Scotland. Although Northern Ireland is not specifically covered, many of the practices and issues are the same (although in Northern Ireland children are in the care of health and social services trusts – not local authorities). Some of the legislation varies slightly between the four nations, and for the sake of simplicity, only major differences between nations will be highlighted here.

This book focuses on people who want to find out more about fostering children in the care of a local authority. Local authorities place children for fostering either with their own foster carers, or with carers recruited by voluntary agencies (such as large children's charities), or with carers recruited by independent fostering providers (IFPs); these may be commercial agencies or not-for-profit organisations. All of these types of fostering agencies are inspected and approved by Government to comply with fostering regulations. For the sake of convenience, the term "fostering agency" is used in this book to refer to the local authority team or voluntary or independent agency staff who recruit foster carers and prepare, train and support them.

In most cases, the child or young person will not be known to the foster carer (which is why this is sometimes referred to as "stranger fostering"). However, in some cases, for example, a residential worker, youth worker or teacher who has formed a close link with a child who needs foster care, might apply to a fostering agency to be considered for this role.

This book does not cover "private fostering", which is a private arrangement made by a child's parents with another person – who might be a friend or someone who has decided to become a private foster carer. Private fostering currently doesn't fall within local authority minimum standards, but all private foster carers must report to their local authority which must visit them and carry out an inspection. This is to ensure that they are adequate for the role. (For more information about private fostering, see BAAF's Advice Note, *Private Fostering,* in Useful Publications). However, it may be very helpful for people considering private fostering to read about agency practices and the implications of caring for someone else's child.

This book will, however, cover some aspects of "family and friends" or "kinship" fostering, which is arranged through a local authority. It is very beneficial for children and young people to be cared for by people they already know. Family and friends wanting to fulfil this role may find this book helpful because it explains the way that

fostering agencies work in partnership with children and their
families, and the expectations they have for people who are caring
for these children. The assessment and preparation of someone to
care for a relative or friend's child, and the financial arrangements
made, may be slightly different to the processes for someone
fostering a child who is not known to them.

It should also be borne in mind that, at the time of writing, there are
changes going on in local authorities with plans for the setting up of
more joint services between social services, education, health and
some other areas. Whilst we have provided a comprehensive list of
fostering agencies at the time of going to press, some changes may
occur and you may need to check these with local directories or by
contacting your local authority on a central number.

Children who need fostering

JOHN BIRDSALL

I like being in care. Where I live now they are kind and loving like a proper mum and dad.
12-year-old fostered boy, *Not Just a Name*, p77

Fostering is usually a temporary arrangement to provide a child with family life when the child can't live with their own family. Many children who are fostered return to their own families although some will stay in foster care for long periods, or may go on to be adopted.

Children of all ages – from babies right through to teenagers – may need to live with foster carers for anything from a single night to several months or several years.

Why do children need fostering?

There can be many reasons why a child or young person needs foster care. It's often because their family is having problems and needs help to sort these out. It might be that the parent is unable to look after the child because of illness or mental health problems. Or the parent may have a drug or alcohol-related problem which seriously affects the safety or care of the child. Or it might be that someone living in the family home has seriously neglected or physically or sexually abused the child.

Sometimes it's because there are major problems in the family and a teenager feels that they need to be away from home for a while. Sometimes a young person has been remanded by a court into foster care. In Scotland they may be required to live in foster care as part of a supervision order. Foster care can also be used as a way of looking after unaccompanied refugee or asylum-seeking children.

Families of disabled children or children with severe behavioural problems may also benefit from short breaks – where the child enjoys time in a new environment and the parents have some time to themselves.

> **My foster parents treat me better than my mum because she was alcoholic. They are capable of looking after me.**
> 14-year-old fostered girl, *Not Just a Name*, p77

Are children from the same family always fostered together?

Children can really benefit from being with their brothers and sisters when other aspects of their family life seem to be turning upside down. So in most cases social workers will try to find foster carers who can look after brothers and sisters together, or if this isn't possible, two foster carers who live near to each other so that siblings can maintain close contact.

Can I foster children from different families at the same time?

You can foster several unrelated children or young people at one time. The regulations in England and Wales say that you should never be fostering more than three unrelated children or young people simultaneously. In Scotland there is no specific requirement. If there are special reasons for you to take more than three unrelated children, a senior officer from the local authority can agree to an exemption.

Do all children who come into foster care have problems?

Most children or young people who need fostering are likely to be experiencing difficulties in their lives. This might be the result of living in a family where there have been tensions and problems, or because the child has been harmed, neglected or frightened. Some children may also feel very angry and confused about the things that have happened to them, and distressed by being separated from their families. Often their behaviour will reflect this. Some may express this in anger, some may become very withdrawn, and some children seem to take all these things in their stride.

Every child is different and reacts differently to the circumstances in which they find themselves. Foster carers receive training to help them think about how to respond to children's needs and to cope with challenging behaviour.

┃ **Disabled children**

Children may need fostering because their parents are finding it hard to cope with their physical or learning disabilities. This may be simply for a short break, perhaps a weekend once a month or the occasional week – which is agreed between the family and the fostering agency. Or the parent may be finding it hard to cope with the child's disabilities and needs a longer period to sort out their own problems, and perhaps learn more about ways to care for their child. Or a child who is disabled has been physically hurt or sexually abused or neglected, and needs to live with a foster carer while plans are made for the child's future – just the same as any other child in such a distressing situation.

Some foster carers specialise in caring for children who have disabilities, such as cerebral palsy, muscular dystrophy or cystic fibrosis. Or they choose to look after children who have a learning disability such as Down's syndrome or a condition like autism.

> **Most of John's problem is that he knows what to say in his brain but can't get it out. He can't connect his brain to what he wants to say and starts to stutter – gets angry because you can't understand and then lashes out. We say, 'Stop, John. Calm down. What do you want to say?' It's knowing John, knowing what he's going to say. Stopping him before he starts – slow down. Then he gets on OK.**
> Foster carer in *Growing up in Foster Care*, p170

┃ **Children's heritage**

Being away from their own families can be a very confusing experience for a child, so wherever possible fostering agencies find foster carers who reflect the child's heritage. It's easier for a child to settle into a foster family which shares the same ethnic background and religion as the child's own family, whose members speak the same language as the child, eat similar food and observe the same customs. There can also be important benefits such as an African foster carer knowing how to care for the hair and skin of an African or African-Caribbean child, and where to find the products most suited for the child's needs. Being with a family from their own community also helps a child to maintain a sense of their identity, and to cope with issues around racism and low self-esteem.

> **I remember when I was a child I had to stay away from home when my mother was ill. When children and young people come to me I see that they are going through those unhappy feelings I went through. I want to help them feel as secure as possible, and in an Asian family which does things in similar ways to their own families.**
> Jane, foster carer

Are there different types of fostering?

Every child is different, so fostering agencies need to recruit a very wide pool of carers who can look after children of different ages and with different needs. Some foster carers specialise in fostering particular groups of children, for example, looking after teenagers on remand, or pre-school children, but other foster carers combine several types.

There are different names given to different types of fostering, which may refer to how long the foster care lasts, e.g. emergency or short-term, or to things such as the age group of the children and young people, or to their particular needs.

| **Types of foster care**

- **emergency** – when children need somewhere safe to stay immediately for a few nights.

- **short-term** – when carers look after children for a few weeks or months, while plans are made for the children's future.

- **long-term** – when a child lives with long-term foster carers until they reach adulthood and are ready to live independently. Not all children who cannot return to their own families want to be adopted, especially older children or those who continue to have regular contact with their relatives.

- **short break** – when disabled children with special needs or children with behavioural problems enjoy a short stay with another family, while their own family or usual foster carers have a short break for themselves. This type of foster care may also be known as respite, family link or shared care.

- **remand fostering** – in England and Wales, when young people are "remanded" by a court into the care of specially trained foster carers. In Scotland, young people may be placed in foster care as an alternative to placement in secure accommodation.

- **treatment foster care** – when foster carers look after children and young people with complex needs and behavioural problems who are also receiving intensive support from therapeutic mental health services.

- **family and friends or kinship** – when children are cared for by people they already know – this can be very beneficial. This is called "family and friends" or "kinship" fostering if it is arranged by the local authority. These arrangements may be different to those for foster carers looking after children who are not previously known to them.

- **sibling groups** – when carers take large groups of brothers and sisters so that siblings aren't separated.

- **mother and baby** – when a carer looks after school-girl mothers and their babies, and helps them to prepare for the future.

- **preparation for adoption** – when a foster carer helps children who cannot return to their own families prepare to move to an adoptive family.

- **support fostering** – sometimes called "community fostering", this is still a relatively new type of foster care. Experienced foster carers provide care for children who are still living in their own families. This care may be provided in the family's own home or in the carer's home.

What is private fostering?

Private fostering is a private arrangement between the parents of a child and a private individual, who may be a friend or someone who has decided to become a private foster carer. This type of fostering doesn't fall within local authority requirements for minimum standards, but all private foster care arrangements must be reported to the local authority, which must make an inspection to ensure that the child is being adequately cared for. Friends can only care for someone else's child for up to 28 days before the situation is classified as private fostering. (BAAF produces an Advice Note, *Private Fostering* (see Useful Publications), which gives more information about this subject.)

What's the difference between fostering and adoption?

Fostering is different from adoption because when a child is in foster care the plan is usually to try and help the child return home. The child's parents also continue to have "parental responsibility" for the child, even if the local authority applies to the courts to stop the parents exercising some of this responsibility.

If it becomes clear that there is no possibility for a child to return home, then attempts will be made to see if anyone else in the family can care for them. If this doesn't happen, the local authority will consider how they can provide a sense of security and "permanence" for the child. For younger children and for those who don't have regular contact with their own families, adoption may be a very good way of providing this.

When you foster a child you take care of the child on a day-to-day basis. You work with the fostering agency and other professionals who are involved in planning for the child's future. You will probably also work with the child's parents. Fostering is a bit like caring for a friend's or relative's child – you provide very high quality care, but you don't encourage the child to see you as a replacement for their own parents.

When a child is adopted, all "parental responsibility" for the child passes to the new family – as though the child had been born into that family. The child continues to be a member of the new family even when they reach adulthood – just as any other child born to that family would be.

Some foster carers adopt children whom they have cared for, but fostering should never be considered as an easy route into adoption. When you approach an agency, you should think very carefully about whether fostering or adoption will be the best option for your family, because the preparation for each is usually a different process.

Who can foster?

JOHN BIRDSALL

> **While you are looked after in foster care you're given a secure and stable environment, with people to help and who are there 24 hours a day and they are familiar.**
> 16-year-old fostered girl, *Not Just a Name*, p77

Who are fostering agencies looking for?

Fostering agencies are looking for people who can provide safe, secure and caring environments for children and young people who are separated from their own families. They need a wide range of people because every child is different and children of all ages need foster carers. They also need people from different walks of life, from different cultures and communities, who can reflect and understand a child's heritage, ethnicity, language and religion.

The role of a foster carer is to work in partnership with the fostering agency and other professionals to help a child prepare to return to their own family, or to move on to adoption or whatever arrangements are being made for the child's long-term needs. Therefore fostering agencies need people who are willing and able to work as part of a team.

What sort of person makes a good foster carer?

To look after someone else's children you need to really like the company of children and enjoy spending time with them – it may seem obvious but it's essential. You must also have plenty of patience and be prepared to get to know the child, and to try and understand the world from their point of view. You also need to be prepared to stick with children through difficult times, and to encourage and support children and young people who have very low self-confidence and may be disillusioned and angry with everything around them.

You will also need to be prepared to work with children's families. Most children who are fostered will return home, and even if they don't, having contact with family and friends often continues to be an important part of their lives. You'll need to understand why children love their own families – even if someone in that family has hurt them badly. So it's important not to be judgemental, but to be prepared to help the child remember good times from the past, as well as help them come to terms with some of the upsetting things that have happened. You will probably be asked to have parents visiting their children in your home, so you need to make them feel welcome, whatever your personal feelings may be about the way they have treated their child. Otherwise you won't be able to help them or their children make things better for the future.

Do I need to have certain skills?

You may hear the word "skills" used a lot in connection with fostering, but it often refers to such practical things as the ability to communicate well with a child or to see the world through a child's eyes. Some people are good at encouraging and praising children and making children feel valued and appreciated. Other very useful skills include being able to calm down a situation which is getting out of hand, and helping a child channel their energy in the right direction. You may have some of these skills already, and others like them, through your own personal experiences. Others can be gained through the training you receive as a foster carer.

Agencies are keen to recruit people who have already worked with children, for example, social workers, teachers and youth workers. But people who have experience of caring for their own children, or for the children of friends and relatives, will also have many skills to offer.

When a fostering agency carries out an "assessment" of you, they will look for the practical skills and abilities you already have. They recognise that there will also be areas in which you feel less confident and need help to develop new skills. For example, you may need to learn more about how to manage challenging behaviour, how to care safely for children who have been sexually abused, or how to work with children's own parents. This is why people interested in fostering are expected to take part in preparation courses, and in ongoing training if they go on to be approved as foster carers.

Assessment

This is the process the fostering agency uses to find out whether fostering is going to be right for you and your family, and what abilities and skills you have to offer to children and young people who are separated from their own families. Sometimes people call this process a "home study", because the social worker visits you in your home, discusses issues such as childcare, families and relationships with you, and asks you to provide evidence of your knowledge of caring for children. The social worker keeps notes about these meetings so they can prepare a detailed report to take to the fostering panel.

Are there age limits?

There are no official age limits for fostering. But a fostering agency will expect you to be mature enough to look after someone else's children, and to work effectively with the child's family, social workers and other professionals involved in their care. However, if you are looking after a child who is related or well known to you ("family and friends" or "kinship" fostering), the agency may be prepared to consider someone younger than the normal age range they would recruit carers from, e.g. a 19-year-old might offer to look after her younger half-brother to keep the family together while their mother is in prison.

Grandparents can make excellent foster carers because of their parenting and grandparenting experience. However, looking after children or young people requires stamina, so the fostering agency will want to know that you are fit and well enough to undertake the task. Some agencies may have established a policy about a "retirement" age.

Do I need to be married?

All sorts of people become foster carers. That includes people who are single or living with a partner (cohabiting), as well as people who are married or divorced. If you are in a relationship, the fostering agency will want to make sure that the relationship is stable, so you can provide security and continuity for the children you look after.

Lesbians and gay men can become foster carers; this may be as a single person or as a couple in England and Wales. In Scotland, fostering regulations prohibit unrelated adults of the same sex living together from being approved as foster carers.

If you are fostering alone, it's important to have a good network of friends and family (although it doesn't need to be both). This is important because you may need to call on people to help out if you get ill or have to drop everything to be somewhere for the child or young person. You will also need people you can turn to for friendship and a chance to unwind, when things aren't going as well as they could. If your friends or family are going to be helping you to care for the child, they will also need to be checked by the fostering agency to make sure they are safe to be around children and have an understanding of the needs of foster children.

> **I didn't realise that single people could foster. I was divorced and I had a child of my own. Then my friend told me about this scheme to recruit foster carers. It's worked out really well for all of us – my son loves having other kids in the house and I get to spend lots of time with children, which I missed when I gave up nursing.**
> Chris, foster carer

> ## I'm going to be doing most of the care. Will my partner also be a "foster carer"?

Some couples foster as a partnership – where they both share equal responsibility for the care of foster children. However, in many situations one of the partners takes on most of the caring responsibilities and the other partner helps out for only part of the time, for example, if the latter is working full-time and the former is at home. In this situation, the fostering agency will still want to make sure that both partners are able to provide high quality, safe care for children.

I have children of my own

Having your own children can be very valuable experience when it comes to fostering. But fostering is a role that the whole family takes on because it has a big impact on family life. It can be a very enjoyable experience for children to have new friends in the house, and many children say they have learnt a lot from it, but there may also be tensions over sharing toys and possessions, or time spent with parents. So the fostering agency will want to know that you have thought about this carefully, and they will talk to your children about their feelings. Some agencies run preparation groups and support groups for sons and daughters of foster carers. BAAF publishes a book, *We are Fostering*, which is useful for children who foster (see Useful Publications).

If you don't have children of your own, then it's important to have some experience of caring for children, before you consider becoming a foster carer. Fostering agencies are keen to recruit people who have professional experience, e.g. teachers, youth workers, social workers or care workers in residential homes, but they are also interested in people who have spent time caring for relatives' or friends' children, or who have worked with children as volunteers, e.g. running a Guide or Scout group or being a sports coach.

> **I suppose because she used to give, like, cuddles, she used to give me a bath and she would, like, read to me the bedtime story and tuck me into bed and things like that, just things like mother things, you know, but because no one had ever done them before, so it was just**

completely like 'wow', you know.
Fostered child, in *Part of the Family*, p168

I'm disabled. Will I be considered?

It can be a very positive experience for a child with a disability to be cared for by someone who shares their disability and understands the problems of growing up disabled. For example, there are many benefits for a Deaf child to be fostered by a family who use the same form of communication, such as British Sign Language, and are a part of Deaf culture. However, it will rather depend on how your disability affects your ability to care for a child. Looking after children requires a certain level of fitness and mobility and you may find that difficult if you have limited mobility or tire easily.

Can we afford to foster? We don't own our house

You don't need to own your own house to be able to foster – but you do need enough space for an extra child. And you don't need to be well-off to be a foster carer – some carers are on benefits. As a foster carer you receive an allowance to cover the cost of having a child living with you, so you should never be out of pocket as a foster carer.

Some fostering agencies run "professional" schemes where carers are classed as self-employed and receive a fee for the work they do. This may be tax-free if it falls below the tax threshold (see Chapter 7).

I have a criminal record

There are some offences that mean you cannot be considered as a foster carer, for example, if you have a conviction or caution under Section 1 of the Sexual Offences Act 1956 (England and Wales), or a conviction or caution for "crimes of violence" against children as listed in Schedule 1 of the Children and Young People Act (England and Wales) 1933. Schedule 1 of the Criminal Procedure (Scotland)

Act 1995 gives information about offences which could bar people from fostering in Scotland.

However, minor offences, especially those committed when you were younger, won't necessarily prohibit you from fostering. But the fostering agency will need to know about these and consider them carefully with your application. Everyone applying to foster has to go through criminal record checks, so it's a good idea to mention any criminal convictions when you first apply to become a foster carer.

| Do I have to be British?

You don't have to be a British citizen to foster in the UK, but you will probably need to prove that you have the right to be "domiciled" in the UK, i.e. the UK is your permanent home and you have the right to stay here permanently.

However, an agency might be prepared to consider someone who is here for a specific period of time, e.g. the partner of someone on a long-term work permit, if the person could prove they would be here for sufficient time to undertake the preparation and training and have children placed with them. This would be more likely to be the case if the person applying can offer support to children from their own country of origin for whom there is a current shortage of carers.

| I'm white but I'm happy | to take black children

Being away from their own families can be a very unsettling experience for children, and wherever possible it's best for children to go to families who reflect their background, ethnicity, language, culture and religion. A black family can also help a black child to cope with experiences of racism and provide positive role models, which are important for developing a child's self-esteem and sense of identity. Agencies are required to place children with families who reflect the child's heritage whenever this is possible.

However, with an emergency unplanned foster placement, the

agency may have no choice but to place a child with foster carers of a different ethnic origin who can take the child at very short notice. If the child remains in foster care, the agency will try to find carers who reflect the child's heritage.

How to go about it

JOHN BIRDSALL

It does feel odd having people ask you so many questions about your life and stuff about your relationships. But if one of my kids was going to someone else, I'd want to make sure they were a hundred and ten per cent OK, so I know it's very important that the social workers find out as much about you as possible.
Peter, foster carer

Becoming a foster carer can be a very rewarding experience, but it's also a very big commitment. So it's a good idea to find out as much as possible about the things agencies are looking for in carers, and the needs of children who come into foster care. BAAF publishes several books about this subject (see Useful Publications).

How do I find a fostering agency?

This important step is fully covered in Chapter 11, followed by a list of fostering agencies in England, Scotland and Wales.

Can I respond to advertisements in my local newspaper or family-finding magazines?

When children and young people appear in local newspapers or magazines such as *Be My Parent* (published by BAAF) or *Foster Care* (published by Fostering Network), it is because their local authority needs to find a family who can offer the child or young person some sort of permanence. This might be with an adoptive parent or with a long-term foster carer. Before any child can join a foster or adoptive family, that family needs to be assessed and approved as suitable to care for children – this is a lengthy process. It will be in the best interests of the child if the local authority can find someone who has already been approved, and is now waiting to be matched to a child who needs foster carers. So it's more common for people wanting to be foster carers to reply to these advertisements after they have been approved by a fostering agency.

But it's always worth making enquiries if you feel that you could match the particular needs of a child or group of siblings, particularly if those needs are unusual or complex. You might be just the family that an agency has been looking for, and they will be willing to take the time to assess your suitability for this child or sibling group.

Can I foster only for my own local authority?

No. You don't have to foster for your own local authority. You can choose to foster for a neighbouring local authority, or for a voluntary agency or independent fostering provider, which cross local authority boundaries. However, it's usually best if children are placed for fostering with people who live close to the child's own family, school, community and friends, so you might find that agencies want to find carers who live in the local area.

But in some circumstances children may need foster places away from their homes, for example, if a disabled child is attending a special residential school and needs to spend weekends and some holidays with a foster family who live nearby, or in cases when it is not safe for a child to remain in their home area.

How do I contact an agency?

You might want to call some of the fostering agencies in your area, or close to your area, which are listed in Chapter 11 of this book, and ask them about the type of foster carers they are looking for. Or you might want to respond to advertisements you see locally or as part of national recruitment campaigns. You might find that not all agencies are looking for the same thing. For example, some might be keen to recruit carers for teenagers because they currently have enough carers for younger children. Others may need carers to look after younger children. Or they may be very short of black carers, or carers from particular ethnic backgrounds, or white carers, who can reflect the backgrounds of the children they need to place.

You should also find out as much as possible about how the agency works and consider which agency is best suited to what you want to get out of fostering. For example, some local authorities and fostering agencies require "professional" or "career" foster carers, and pay fees to people who have or are prepared to develop the specialist knowledge and skills required to look after children with more complex needs. These might include teachers, social workers, youth workers and residential workers as well as other people who can demonstrate the necessary level of relevant experience or skills for this work. (Remember that training will be available.)

But some carers choose to remain as "volunteers" (i.e. they receive an allowance to cover the costs of having the child in their family, but no fees) and foster for their local authority because they feel that this is an important way to support children in their own community. It is important that you think about what type of fostering you might want to consider and collect as much written information as possible from agencies. And don't be afraid to ask questions.

> **I knew she only acted like that because that was the way she'd been treated herself. So we decided to keep her, because she'd had a rough deal – and she deserved a chance.**
> Jane, foster carer, *Foster Care*, issue 115

What happens next?

Some fostering agencies hold open evenings or similar information events, and you may be invited to attend one of these. Or you may simply be sent information through the post at the initial stage.

The second stage is usually a visit from a social worker from the fostering agency. Or in some cases, it may be an experienced foster carer who comes to see you. Some agencies find that people are more comfortable talking to a foster carer at this point because they feel they can ask more questions. But whoever comes to visit, make sure you use this as an opportunity to ask about anything that you want to know. For example, if you are worried that you might not be able to afford to foster then ask about the financial side of things. Or if you are worried that a criminal conviction might stand in the way, tell the social worker at this early stage. It's much better to talk about these things early on, rather than waste your time if something is going to be a bar to you fostering.

At this stage, the social worker will explain to you what is involved in fostering and the "assessment" process, and describe the preparation you will need to go through to be considered. If you want to go ahead with applying, you will be asked to fill in an application form (a sample is included at the back of this book). You will be required to give details about yourself, your partner (if you have one), and other people living in your home. You will also be asked to give permission for the agency to carry out police checks, so that they can make sure you and any other people living with you do not have a conviction for offences against children, and that a child will be safe living with you. You will also be asked to have a health check to show that you don't have any major health problems that would make it difficult for you to look after children and young people. The names and details of people who are prepared to give references about you will also be needed.

| **Preparation**

Once you start the process of applying to be a foster carer, you will be asked to attend preparation sessions to learn more about fostering and what's involved. Other people who are applying to foster will also be attending these sessions, and there's usually a chance to meet and hear about the experiences of people who are experienced foster carers. These sessions cover important issues, such as understanding how children feel when they are separated from their own families; working with children's parents; child protection issues and how to provide "safe" care; and managing difficult behaviour. These groups also help you to think about the fact that you are caring for someone else's child, and how you will prepare to say "goodbye" when the child is ready to move on.

> **The preparation group was much better than we'd imagined. It was good to be in the same boat as other people, all of us not really knowing what to expect and being able to talk about things without**

> **feeling like you were getting it wrong or
> asking stupid questions. We've stayed
> friends with one of the couples we met
> in the group.**
> Savita, foster carer

Safe care

Safe care is the term used to describe ways of looking after
children and young people, which protect the child or young
person from situations which may remind them of times when
they have been abused, or which they may misinterpret as
being abusive. Safe care is also about the carer making sure
that they protect themselves from a child or young person
making allegations against them by carefully considering their
actions in order to avoid this kind of misunderstanding. Foster
carers are taught about safe care as part of their preparation
and training.

Assessment

You will also receive a series of visits from a social worker, who
will help you to think about the skills that you will need. They will
help you to look at your own life experiences, your knowledge of
caring for children and young people, and how you would work as
part of a team. They will also help you to identify areas where you
might need extra training or support. If you have your own children,
the social worker will ask them how they feel about the idea of other
children living in their home. Some fostering agencies also run
groups for the sons and daughters of people applying to become
foster carers, to help them prepare to become part of a family who
fosters.

Your social worker will record information about you as part of the
process, and will use this to put together a report which brings
together all the information they have gathered about you. This gives
details of your skills, and your social worker's recommendations
about the age of children or type of fostering they feel you will be
best suited to. They also include details of any areas where they feel

you will need extra support or training. You will have a chance to see this report and to add your own comments. Sometimes people prepare their own information to add to the application, e.g. some families make a tape, or their children write their own comments about why they think their family will be good as foster carers.

Will they ask very personal questions?

The social worker will want to build up a picture of you and your family (if you have one). They will want to know what is important to you, and the experiences that have made you into the person you are now. So, for example, they will ask about your own experiences of childhood and your attitudes towards discipline, and things like building up children's self-confidence and how to communicate with children. They will also want to know about your relationships – with your partner (if you have one), with your children (if you have any), and with relatives and friends.

They may ask about intimate areas of your life because this can be relevant to how you care for a child or young person. This might seem very intrusive, but you have to try and see it from their point of view. You might be asked to think about a recent bereavement you have had and how you will cope with a child who has experienced major losses in their life. Or if you and your family tend to walk about the house with very few clothes on, you will be asked to consider the effect on a child who has been sexually abused in the past.

You might also be asked to think about what advice you would give to a young person who thinks they are gay, lesbian or bisexual, or who is under the age of consent and having sex. And if there are problems in your sexual relationship, what might be the effect of looking after a teenager who behaves provocatively towards you or your partner?

It's much better to get issues out into the open and think about how you would deal with them at this stage, rather than wait until later on when they might cause problems. Talking about these situations can also help you to think about the best ways to provide "safe care" to children and young people, so that a child isn't placed in a situation where they might misunderstand your intentions and make an allegation that you have behaved inappropriately.

But if you do find some of these matters really difficult to speak about (for example, because, in your culture, these issues are never discussed with strangers), explain this to the social worker. Ask for time to think about the issues on your own or with your partner, and ask the social worker to be more specific about why they need to know this information.

Who makes the decision about whether I'm suitable?

When the report is ready, you social worker will present it to a fostering panel. Every agency has its own fostering panel, although a few share their panel with a neighbouring agency. This is a group of people with a combination of professional and personal experiences of fostering. The panel may include very experienced social workers, who are different to the social workers who have helped you prepare your application; foster carers or people who have grown up in foster care; and representatives from the local community, such as councillors. Panels also have legal and medical advisers who help them in the decision-making process.

The panel receives information about your application before the meeting so they have time to consider this carefully. The panel is expected to respect the confidentiality of applicants and will only discuss relevant information with other members of the panel during the panel meeting. During the meeting, they discuss the positive things you have to offer as well as any concerns they may have about your suitability as a carer. The social worker who carried out your assessment will attend the meeting so that they can answer any questions the panel has. In Scotland, it is usual for applicants to be invited to attend the panel. In England and Wales, some panels invite people applying to foster to attend the panel, but some feel that this makes panel members more inhibited about raising concerns they may have if the person they are considering is present.

When the panel has reached a decision, they then make a recommendation to a senior member of the fostering agency. It is this senior person in the agency who makes the ultimate decision, based on the recommendation made by the panel. This agency decision worker will write to you with their decision. Your social worker will explain to you why the panel has made its recommendation and will discuss this with you.

The role of a fostering panel

The fostering panel is made up of professionals and individuals with considerable knowledge of fostering. They must carefully consider your suitability to offer safe, high quality care to children, and your ability to meet the needs of a particular age group of children, or for any specific type of fostering you are applying to be considered for. But the panel does not make the ultimate decision – it simply makes a recommendation which is passed on to a senior member of the fostering agency. It is very rare – but not completely unknown – for a panel's recommendation to be rejected by the agency's decision-maker, but this can happen in exceptional circumstances. Applicants are given reasons why their application to foster has been turned down.

Do people sometimes get turned down?

If your social worker feels that fostering isn't going to be right for you, or that this is not the right time for you to consider it, then they will try and explain this to you. So in most cases, people only go forward to panel if both they and their social worker are confident that they have something very positive to offer.

However, there are always minuses as well as pluses in any family.

As a family, you may have great skills and a wealth of experience to offer a child, but there might also be some other factors that need to be taken into account, for example, possible changes on the horizon, such as an older relative who may need care or your grown-up child returning home after a divorce. These changes might affect the time you are able to spend with a child, so the panel might have to consider carefully whether the positive points outweigh the negative points.

What if I don't agree with the decision?

If you are not approved, you should receive a written notice with reasons and a copy of the panel's recommendation, and be invited to submit any written representations within 28 days.

If you wish to appeal against the decision, you must write to the agency decision maker within 28 days. A different panel to the one which considered your original application must give further consideration to your application. You will probably be invited to attend the panel to discuss this and to put forward any further information you want the panel to consider. You will probably be allowed to bring someone with you to support you.

The panel will then make another recommendation, taking into account what you have said and any new information they have considered. They may uphold their previous recommendation or make a new one. The decision will then be taken by the senior member of the agency, and you will be notified and given a written explanation if you have been turned down again.

If you are still unhappy and feel you have been unfairly treated, you may decide to make use of the agency's complaints procedures.

Can I apply again or to another agency?

If your circumstances change substantially in the future, it may be appropriate for you to apply to the same agency again. Or you may want to apply to another agency which needs foster carers for different types of children and different types of situations. For example, some agencies particularly need foster carers to provide "short break" care – where foster carers have children to stay with them at weekends or for holiday periods. It might be that an agency which needs people for this type of fostering won't be so concerned that you have some important commitments on your time, so long as you can make a major commitment for the two weekends a month (or whatever period is agreed) that the child is staying with you. But agencies may ask you whether you have applied elsewhere, and it's best to be honest with them about any reasons you have been given for being turned down.

How long does it take to go through the assessment process?

Deciding to foster is a decision that shouldn't be rushed, and most agencies will take at least six months before they feel you are ready for your report to be taken to a fostering panel. Sometimes it can take a lot longer than this because there are no social workers available to assess you, or because you need to wait until the next preparation course starts. Or it might be because you or your family need longer to think about what is involved in fostering.

However, if you feel that an agency has simply forgotten about your application or is taking an unreasonable time to contact you, don't be afraid to contact them. They are probably very busy and may simply have overlooked the fact that you are waiting to hear from them. Be persistent!

Do I get approved for fostering children of all ages?

Most foster carers are approved for fostering a particular age group of children, for example, pre-school children, school-age children, or teenagers. Some foster carers are also approved for particular types of fostering, for example, fostering young people on remand, or caring for children with severe behavioural problems, or taking large groups of brothers and sisters. When you are being assessed by your social workers, you will discuss the type of children you feel you are best suited to care for and your social worker will include this as part of your application to the fostering panel.

Becoming part of the fostering team

JOHN BIRDSALL

I enjoy working with the adults as much as the child. If I had my own children and I was at home with them all day, it would drive me mad. But you go to meetings and get involved with the plans and decisions and you're always working towards things. It's brilliant.

Foster carer, in *Growing up in Foster Care*, p95

Being approved as a foster carer means becoming part of an agency's fostering team and working in partnership with social workers, as well as teachers, medical staff, counsellors and anyone else involved in planning for the child's future and helping the child. The child's own parents will also be consulted and involved in this process, and you may find yourself working with them directly.

Under the law, fostering agencies have duties they must follow. These cover such things as the suitability of foster placements, visiting foster children in foster placements, and requirements for foster carers in carrying out their roles. They also have to follow minimum standards which are set out in legislation in the different UK countries. These standards set out requirements for the way children must be cared for, and how foster carers must work with the agency and the child's family. They also cover the obligations the fostering agency has towards the foster carers.

So you will need to have an understanding of what the agency expects from you, and how you will be expected to work as part of the fostering team.

| Who is in this team?

There are the social workers who work for the local authority or fostering agency you are fostering for. There are also social workers for the child. But you may also work closely with the child's teachers and other specialist staff from the school or education authority – such as the Special Educational Needs Co-ordinator (SENCO) or the designated teacher (someone appointed by the school to look after the needs of children in care). You may need to help school staff understand the difficulties your foster child has, which may be causing behavioural problems. You may also be working alongside health professionals such as GPs, nurses and hospital consultants, and speech and language therapists. If a child has experienced a lot of emotional trauma and disruption, they may also need to see a therapist or counsellor. You may be asked to take part in progress meetings with the therapist.

If you have to go to court about your foster child, you may meet the children's guardian (England and Wales) or curator *ad litem* (Scotland), who is appointed by the court to safeguard the interests of the child. They may be interested in your opinions about the choices for the child's future.

The foster carer's social worker

Once you are approved, you will be allocated your own social worker, who might be a different person to the worker who prepared you and took your report to panel. This social worker is usually called the supervising social worker (or sometimes the link worker or support worker). They will contact you to discuss the possibility of a new child being placed with you and the tasks and goals they want you to work to with this child. They will make sure that you receive any additional training or access to aids and equipment that you will need to help you care for the child.

Your supervising social worker will contact or visit you regularly, to make sure that all is going well with the new child and that you are working within the plan that has been agreed for the child. You will be able to discuss any problems or concerns you have with them.

The child's social worker

Children who come to stay with you will also have their own social worker. The child's social worker is the link between the foster carer and the child's family. They will tell you as much as possible about the child or young person's daily routines, cultural or religious practices, dietary needs, and any other special needs or behavioural problems the child may have, before the child moves in with you. They will work with you to make arrangements for the child to have regular contact or visits with their family, and try to resolve any problems that arise from this.

The child's social worker also prepares the child (if the child is old enough) for meetings where plans for their future will be discussed, and helps the child think about the points they want to get across. The social worker will attend the meetings with the child, and as a foster carer you will also be included in most of these meetings. The child's social worker also has to make sure that the child or young person has information about being in foster care, has opportunities to express their opinions and concerns, that their education and health are being looked after, and that they have access to leisure and career opportunities. A lot of this work will be done in close collaboration with you as the foster carer. If the young person is coming up to the age of leaving foster care, they will be helped to prepare for life as a young adult. This work may be undertaken by a social worker who specialises in preparing children who are leaving care, and again you will be involved in this.

> **Our social worker is very good. Sometimes I've got a lot on after school with the other children and I can ring Linda and she will take Andy to contact for me. Anything we need, she'll do it for us. I try to do most things on my own because he's a permanent placement. But it's good to know that Linda's always there for us.**
> Foster carer, in *Growing up in Foster Care*, p83

| Other foster carers

You may also receive support from experienced foster carers. In some agencies, experienced carers "mentor" new foster carers. In many areas there are also fostering associations where you can meet up with other foster carers to exchange ideas, give each other support and maybe do some fun things together – like taking children out for the day as part of a large group, or holding parties and barbeques.

What about the child's parents?

Often fostering is about providing somewhere safe for the child to live while their family receives help to sort out their problems. This might mean the parent having time to go on a rehabilitation course for a drug or drink problem, or to receive treatment for a mental health problem, or for a family to think about how they will keep the child safe in the future. Or it may be a chance for a stressed parent who had little love and support in their own childhood to learn more about how to care for their child. In all these cases, it will be important for the child to continue to have contact with their family so that they will be able to return home as soon as the parents are ready to care for them again. So the child's parents will probably visit them in your home, and be involved in meetings about planning the child's future.

As a member of the fostering team you will be expected to help the child's social worker assess whether parents are ready to resume care of their children.

Will I have to agree anything in writing?

You will usually be required to sign a "general foster care agreement" when you are approved, and then a "placement agreement", to say you have understood the work that the agency is asking you to do with the child. You will be able to discuss with your supervising social worker anything that you don't understand or agree with.

Attending meetings

As a foster carer, you will be expected to attend and contribute to meetings about the child's future. These meetings usually include the child's social workers, other professionals – such as a teacher or child psychologist – and the child's parents. If the child or young person is old enough they may also attend some of these meetings, or they will be helped to express their views before the meetings. These meetings are used to put together a plan for the child's future.

| Attending court

There may be times when you will be asked to attend court to give evidence to help the court reach decisions about the child's future. This might be something positive like the good progress you have seen in a parent's ability to look after their child. Or it may be less positive, perhaps about the way you have seen a family member mistreat a child, or the signs of an injury you have seen. This might sound rather scary, but you will be offered extra help and support to do this. You might be attending court to give support to a child or young person who is giving evidence against an abuser, or telling the judge their feelings about their future. In Scotland, you will be entitled to attend hearings about the young person in your care. Or you may be giving support to a child or young person who is themselves facing a charge, for example, for shoplifting or joyriding.

| Does anyone make sure
| I'm doing a good job?

Your supervising social worker will contact you regularly, and visit you, to see how you are getting on. This will be to offer you support, but also to make sure you are fulfilling your part of the plans for the child's future. Every foster carer also has to have an annual review where the agency checks that you are working within the regulations and standards every agency has to follow, and within any local policies or practices they want you to observe. It's also an opportunity for you and the agency to recognise the new skills you've gained and the positive work you've been doing with children. It's a time to look at whether you are ready to take on more complex or challenging placements, or if there are particular areas where you'd like to develop your knowledge and experience.

However, if you consistently fail to meet requirements and the agency feels that they are no longer able to work with you, the fostering panel might decide to "de-regulate"/"de-register" you so you can no longer foster for them. This may also happen between reviews if you are involved in a serious breach of agency regulations, or if there are concerns about your safety to care for children.

Respecting confidentiality

As a foster carer, you will be given personal information about children and their families. As part of your role, you will be expected to respect confidentiality and not share this information with anyone who is not directly involved in working with the child.

Will I get support if I'm finding things difficult?

Your supervising social worker will contact you to check how things are going with the child they have placed with you. They should be able to offer you advice, extra training, or support if you feel you need help with managing particular aspects of a child's behaviour. Your agency will also have an "out of hours" number you can call if you are having problems, and some have helplines just for foster carers.

You may also find it very helpful to talk to other foster carers who have had similar experiences, and it can be a good idea to join your local foster carer association (see Useful Organisations). Some foster carers are "paired" with a more experienced carer whom they can contact whenever they want to talk something through.

It's also important to have support from your relatives and friends. You won't be able to share detailed information with them about a child's background (because you must respect the child's and family's confidentiality), but you will be able to talk to them about general problems you are facing. Or simply spend some time with them relaxing and doing something completely different!

What happens if I really can't cope with a particular child?

All relationships are about how well human beings get on together, and it's inevitable that there are going to be some children who settle well in your home, and some who don't. You may find that you can see through a short-term foster placement that isn't working very well, if you get the right type of support. But sometimes both you and the child or young person can see that this isn't going to work. In such cases, it's best to be honest with your supervising social worker – for everyone's sake.

Admitting that a particularly difficult foster placement isn't working for you doesn't mean that you have "failed", or that your agency won't be prepared to place other children with you. You might find that caring for children of a certain age group doesn't work for your family because of clashes with your own children, so you and your supervising social worker might discuss whether it would be better for you to take older/younger children in future.

What if I decide I don't want to foster any more?

If you've had a foster placement that has been particularly difficult for you and your family, you might need a break before another child comes to live with you. But many foster carers say they find that after a difficult placement, having the next child feels much easier, and helps to restore their confidence. However, if you give things a try and then realise that fostering isn't right for you and your family, then you need to tell your supervising social worker.

Some people foster for long periods and then decide that it's time for a break, because their circumstances have changed. Some experienced foster carers take a break from fostering but use their time to train and support other foster carers. If you leave fostering through a voluntary decision you can always reapply in the future, when you feel the time might be right for you to consider it again.

Caring for children in your home

> **Whichever of us picks him up from school, his face lights up, he'll see you across the playground. And he'll run up to you and wrap his arms around you – it's lovely.**
> Foster carer, in *Growing up in Foster Care*, p212

There may be a time gap after you have been approved, because the fostering agency doesn't have a child whom they need to place with you just at the moment. But sometimes you may find yourself caring for a child almost immediately, as soon as you are approved. Everyone's experience is different! In some instances you may be asked to attend more training to help you prepare for a particular child or young person coming to stay with you.

What happens when my agency wants me to take a child?

Your supervising social worker will contact you and tell you about a child – or sibling group, if you are prepared to take brothers and sisters – who needs fostering. They will give you an outline of the child or young person's circumstances and the problems and issues they are likely to have. If you are prepared to take this child, then the child's social worker will contact you and give you more information about their daily routines, their school, the types of food they eat, and any medical or special needs they have.

This social worker will also tell you about the child or young person's relationship with members of their own family and whether the child will be having contact with them while they are with you. They will discuss the arrangements for this contact with you, and then oversee it and help you if there are problems. They will explain the "work" they want you to do with the child.

In most cases, children's moves into foster care are planned; in other words, they are discussed beforehand and the child's family is aware of what is happening. So social workers are able to prepare the foster carers to look after the child. But sometimes children come into care on an "emergency" basis. This may be because children are found at home on their own at night; the child's parent is rushed into hospital; the parent is arrested; or the child is considered to be at serious risk of imminent harm.

What if I don't think this child will fit in with my family?

If you feel that this child or young person isn't right for your family, or you feel that there are aspects of the child's needs that you don't feel skilled enough to cope with, you should tell your social worker. They may offer you extra training or support to help you care for the child. You do not have to take any child that you feel you cannot care for. But, obviously, if you turn down every child you are asked to take, then your agency may start to wonder why you have applied to foster!

Will I get information about the child and their family?

You should be given something called a "placement agreement", with details of the child's routines, their needs and the contact they will have with their family. This will also explain the plan for the child and the work that the agency is expecting you to do with the child. You will also be given information about the child or family which is relevant to the care of the child, for example, if the parent has a drug or alcohol problem that has affected the child in the womb.

Won't children be upset and frightened when they first come to me?

Children may be very confused and frightened when they first come to you – especially if their move into care has been a very sudden one. But even if it has been planned, the child may still be very upset or angry. Children love their own families, and even if other adults feel that the child's parents have let them down or harmed them, most children will be unhappy to be away from them. They may also be worrying about brothers or sisters who are still at home, or they may be concerned about a parent who, for example, has a drug or alcohol problem. But some children will arrive seeming very confident and relaxed. They may have been in foster care before and know what to expect!

Your preparation to become a foster carer will help you to think about these issues and how you will help a child to settle in your home. Experienced foster carers say that it's important to take time to show the child or young person around your home, and explain to them where things are and any routines, rules or boundaries that you and your family have. Many carers keep toys, clothes and toiletries to hand in case children or young people have come without their own. If you have children of your own, they often help a new child to settle in. Pets can also be a great way of helping children to relax.

⊺ "Working" with children

The child's social worker will explain to you the "work" that you are expected to do with the child. This means that, in addition to making sure that the child is fed, clothed, kept warm and well looked after in your home, you will help the child with their emotional, practical, educational and developmental needs.

⊺ Emotional needs

Most children in foster care have been through difficult times and some may be very traumatised by their experiences. Their self-confidence is often very low and they may have many worries about the future. Some children will receive professional help from a therapist or psychologist, and many children carry out work around these issues with their social worker. But as a foster carer, you will also be expected to help the child to talk about their memories, fears and worries – as well as to remember good things that have happened to them. You may find yourself doing "life work" (sometimes called "life story work") with a child. This is where you help the child to put together a book about their past. This may include photos or drawings of the people and places that are important to them, to help them talk about and make sense of what has happened in their lives. BAAF has a book for children to use, a CD-ROM, and a guide for adults that explains more (see Useful Publications).

Much of your "work" will be around getting to know the child or young person, so that they feel comfortable about talking to you. Only then will you be able to help them think about ways to tackle problems that are worrying them. You will also help to build up the child or young person's self-esteem by offering encouragement and giving lots of praise when they achieve things – however small.

Sometimes children will "disclose" to you abuse that has happened to them. As part of your training to become a foster carer, you will learn how to help children when they talk about these issues and how to keep records of any information that you need to pass on to the child's social worker.

| Behaviour management

Some of the children you care for may seem just like any other child, well behaved some of the time, difficult some of the time and somewhere in the middle for the rest! But many children and young people in foster care will have problems with their behaviour that they need help with. They may be quiet, withdrawn and anxious. They may self-harm by cutting themselves, or starve themselves, or binge on food. Or they may "fly off the handle" at the slightest provocation, get into fights with other children, or regularly get themselves into trouble at school or with the police.

> I don't try to get them to change really. I think if you can show the child, regardless of how much they're flinging at you, an acceptance, a knowledge – 'I know what you're doing is really rotten but I can understand why you're doing it. I canny change it but maybe I can help you accept it.' And in doing that you might give them the ability to change...you just make them see it in a different light than they did. If

> **there's any changing they have to do it themselves.**
> Foster carer, in *Testing the Limits of Foster Care*, p126

Your job as a foster carer is to help these children and young people start to find different ways to behave. (Your training and preparation as a foster carer, and the additional training and support you receive from your family placement worker, will help you to build up the skills and knowledge to do this.) You will need to help the children understand why they behave as they do in the first place – which is usually because they have no other way of expressing the hurt, anger and frustration that is inside them. And you will need to help them think about alternative ways to get those feelings across, and maybe plan some strategies which they can use when things are difficult for them. These can be as simple as showing a child how to count from ten backwards when they think they are about to explode! Older children may need to develop more confidence and self-respect, to help them stay away from friends who lead them into activities like drug-taking or shoplifting.

| Education

You must make sure that the child is attending school, and you will be expected to attend parents' evenings and other meetings connected with the child's education. Wherever possible, children will attend their usual school but, together with the child's social worker, you may have to identify a new school and help the child settle into this. You will also be expected to make sure that the child receives help with homework. Together with the child's social worker, teachers and education specialists, you will need to make sure that the child gets help with any problems they are experiencing. Some children may be excluded from school and will have lessons with a home tutor or attend a pupil referral unit. Or the child you are caring for may have learning or physical disabilities and attend a special school, which is adapted to their needs.

I was a rebel at school – getting suspended because of what was happening at home. Since I came into care I have matured, I am now at college and take pride in my work.
17-year-old fostered girl, *Not Just a Name*, p34

Working with families

As a foster carer, part of your role will be to help the child maintain contact with their family. This can mean that parents will come to visit their child in your home. You will find yourself talking to parents and helping them to understand more about their child and the best way to care for them. For example, you might invite a parent to join you for a mealtime so they can see how you cope with a child's behaviour when the child refuses to eat food or to sit at the table. Or you might suggest that a mother stays to put her baby to bed, so that you bath the baby together and she can see how you play with and handle the baby as you do this.

Other relatives such as grandparents, cousins, aunts and uncles and close family friends may also visit children in your home, or meet with them in places like restaurants, parks or specialist "contact" centres. The children you care for may also have contact with some family members in their homes, or at the houses of other foster carers who are looking after their brothers and sisters.

Won't it be difficult working with parents who have hurt or neglected their children?

Often when parents neglect their children it is because they have huge problems in their own lives, or they are affected by a mental health problem, or a drug or alcohol problem. And under pressure, a parent may find themselves taking out their own anger and frustration on their child. Or a mother who is suffering domestic abuse herself may be unable to protect her child from her abusive partner. Some parents have had very difficult and abusive childhoods themselves and can lack a basic understanding of what children need in the way of care and stimulation. Many parents do love their children but their lives have become so mixed up that they fail to care for or protect them properly.

As you meet parents of the children you care for, you will find that many of them may talk to you about their lives. This will help you to understand more about why a parent has neglected or hurt their child or allowed someone else to hurt the child. Even if you find it hard not to judge a parent because of the way they have behaved, you will need to hide your feelings for the sake of the child, who probably still loves their parent very deeply.

If you have worries about the way a parent or other relative treats the child, you should talk to the child's social worker about this.

> **Most of the parents don't recognise the neglect they show, because often it was how they were treated themselves when they were kids. So if we can intervene, and help them escape from that process, then that's really valuable.**
> Angie, foster carer, *Foster Care*, issue 113

What happens if a child tells me about sexual abuse?

Children and young people often take time before they feel comfortable enough to reveal sexual abuse or serious or upsetting incidents in their life to their foster carers. It's very important not to show the child you are shocked or disgusted by what they tell you, although you do need to tell them that you think it's very wrong that someone has treated them in this way. You will also need to explain to the child that you cannot keep something so important a secret and you will have to talk to their social worker about this – to make sure that they remain safe in future and to prevent other children from being harmed. During your preparation to foster, you will receive training on how to cope with situations where children disclose abuse to you.

How will I learn to let go when a child leaves?

As a foster carer, unless you are a permanent carer for a child, your role is a temporary one – you are not there to replace the child's own parents. But even so, it can be hard to say goodbye to a child or young person you have cared for. Experienced foster carers say that what helps them most is knowing that the child is happy to be going home to their own parents, or that the child is going on to a new family who can provide permanence and stability for the child. Sometimes children stay in touch with their foster carers after they leave – especially if they have lived with the family for a long time.

> **I like it when the children tell me their worries and I can help them. I love having so many children sharing our house. I write to some of the children who have stayed here and we never forget them.**
> Amelia, child whose family fosters, *Foster Care*, issue 110

Children's feelings about being in foster care

JOHN BIRDSALL

I think foster carers make it as good as possible for you in care as they can. They let us into their home and they look after us almost like their own children.

14-year-old fostered boy, *Not Just a Name*, p78

Imagine how you'd feel if you had got up one morning in your own home, with your own possessions and your own family around you, but by the evening you went to bed in a totally different place, with strangers around you, and not knowing when you'd see your own family again. It's hard enough to cope with this situation as an adult, but imagine how difficult this is for a child!

How do children feel about coming into foster care?

Many children will be confused and rather scared. Others may be angry, withdrawn or just very sad and tearful. You may find that some children and young people who have been in foster care before may seem to take it in their stride, showing few emotions. You may also come across children or young people who are relieved to be away from a difficult situation at home. Every child is different and it's impossible to predict how a change of circumstances will affect them. However, you can be fairly sure that the majority of children will miss their own families a great deal and be keen to return home as soon as possible, however much they enjoy living with you.

> **When I first came to live with the family, I was scared...but now I'm happy. I want to live here forever.**
> Lisa, fostered child, *Foster Care*, issue 115

What if their own families have mistreated them?

Most children continue to love their own families, no matter what has happened. They may not like the way someone in the family has behaved towards them, and they may be frightened of a particular person who has been living in the household, but overall they will continue to feel the strong bond to their family which is experienced by most human beings. Preparation for fostering will help you to think more about the feelings of children and young people towards their families, by asking you to think about the importance of relationships in your own life.

What benefits do children get from fostering?

As a foster carer, you can play an important role in helping a child regain confidence and hope for the future. You will also be able to offer the child a period of stability and support to make sense of things that have happened to them in the past, and to help them prepare for whatever the future holds for them. Sometimes you may feel that you haven't achieved very much with a child, but it's amazing how many young people who have left foster care speak about something relatively small their foster carers did or said, which made a helpful impression on their lives.

Another very important role that foster carers have is to give encouragement and praise to children and young people. Children with low self-confidence can really benefit from being with someone who praises them for small achievements, encourages them to make the best of their educational and other opportunities, and makes them feel worthwhile and valued. This sort of support can be vital in helping a young person to turn their life around.

> **If you can't be with your own mum and dad, you want to be with people who take the time to understand you, listen to you, put up with you when you're behaving like a right pain. You might get fed up with them at the time, nagging you to do homework and the like, but then you look back and you wouldn't have got to college or whatever if they didn't believe in you and want you to do well.**
> Jack, young person who was fostered

Will children want to call us mum and dad?

Many children who are fostered will be going home to their own families, or continue to have regular contact with them. So it could be very confusing for the child – and very hurtful for their own parents – if the child starts thinking about you as replacements for their own mum and dad. So you will need to discuss with them what they are going to call you. Perhaps you will decide to use your first name.

But if we're long-term foster carers, won't the child become part of our family?

If you become long-term carers for a child who really can't return home to their family, then it is likely that the child will begin to feel like part of your family. You'll get to know each other well and share many of the day-to-day things that families share with each other, as well as special things like holidays and family celebrations. But the child will probably continue to have contact with their own parents, brothers and sisters, and other relatives, and will want to phone them and talk about them. It can help to think about how you would look after a friend's child if the friend died or was permanently unable to look after them. You would provide love and care and support for the child, but at the same time would want the child to know about their own parents.

Will children I foster want to stay in touch or come back and see me?

Some children will want to stay in touch with you and your children, especially if they have lived with you for a long period and you have built up a good relationship with them. You might find that some young people continue to visit you when they are adults – bringing their own children to see you!

Others will only stay with you for a short time and you may not see or hear from them after they leave. This is why it is important for foster carers to put together a little book of photographs with details and mementos of things the child has done while they were with them. This can help the child to make sense of things that have happened in their lives. This can help to prevent a young person growing up wondering about the name of the family with the black cat and the funny shaped garden, or where the beach was that they got the pebble from on the day it rained – because you have put all that information in a scrapbook and put the pebble in a box for them.

7

Getting practical: money, training, careers and dealing with problems

JOHN BIRDSALL

I've always loved children and I wanted to foster when I was a wee girl. But getting paid helps. It makes you feel you're appreciated and doing a proper job.
Sian, foster carer

| Is fostering a job?

Traditionally, fostering was seen as a voluntary service – that is, something that people did because they wanted to help children in their local community. Today, it's recognised that foster carers need to bring many skills to their role, and to work as professionals who are part of the fostering team. Some foster carers continue to see themselves as volunteers, but others see themselves as truly "professional" and make fostering a career. This is usually determined by the type of fostering they do, the agency they work for, and the level of skills and experience they can offer.

> **There are kids who fit really well into your family and are easy to care for. Then there's the kids you want to like but you can't help but think, when is this kid leaving us? Still, you do your best for all of them 'cos that's what you're doing it for, and you want to do a good job every time.**
> Russ, foster carer

| Do foster carers get paid?

Everyone who fosters receives an allowance to cover the cost of caring for a child or young person in their own home. This is set by the individual fostering agency and usually depends on the age of the child. This is meant to cover basics like food and clothes, but also other costs such as taking a child to medical appointments, or attending meetings about plans for the child's future. (Fostering Network produces an annual guide, *Foster Care Finance*, which recommends the basic level of allowances it believes foster carers should receive for different ages of children – see Useful Organisations.)

These days, many fostering agencies run "professional" schemes which pay a fee to foster carers. These schemes usually require the foster carer to have a certain level of skills and experience of working with children, and are often connected with specialist types of fostering, e.g. fostering young people who are on remand, or caring for children with particularly challenging behaviour. These fees may increase as the foster carer develops new levels of skill.

Some independent fostering providers employ foster carers in similar ways to other employers. This might include paying carers for holiday periods when the foster carer has no child living with them. Many foster carers who receive a fee are classed as "self-employed".

Do foster carers pay tax?

Recently UK law was changed by the Finance Act 2003, so that foster carers who are paid or receive a fee do not pay tax on their income from fostering, up to a maximum of £10,000, plus the allowances they receive to cover the costs of having a child to live with them.

Can foster carers claim benefits?

If you are on a low income, you may still be able to claim benefits such as working families tax credit and housing benefits. But this may depend on whether you receive a fee for fostering and how the fee is made up. Some high-paying fees may take you above the threshold for benefits. If you are worried about whether you can afford to foster and how fostering might affect your benefits, you should ask about this when you first apply.

What about pensions?

Since the law changed in 2003, foster carers are now entitled to Home Responsibility Protection (HRP). HRP is a benefit for people who might otherwise lose their pension because they have given up work to look after a child (or a sick or disabled person). Before April 2003 it was not available to people caring for someone else's child.

What happens if a child damages my home?

Usually agencies have a corporate insurance scheme, or they pay for their carers to belong to an insurance scheme. You should ask your fostering agency about the arrangements they will make to cover you for any loss or damage, and what arrangements you may need to make with your own household insurance company.

Do I get opportunities to develop my skills or gain qualifications as a foster carer?

As a foster carer, you will be expected to attend training to update your skills and help you respond to children whose needs may be more challenging than you are used to. This training will also help to ensure that you meet the national minimum standards for foster carers. Some fostering agencies also offer carers the chance to gain a national qualification, such as an NVQ level 3 Caring for Children and Young People in England and Wales, or an SVQ in Scotland. Experienced foster carers may also be offered opportunities to mentor and train other foster carers.

> **Getting the training in managing difficult behaviour was a big help. We had this lad who was – I don't know, up and down all the time. Like a pot boiler. After the training I had these new ideas, and more confidence, and some of them really worked for him.**
> Barry, foster carer

8

The law, regulations and requirements

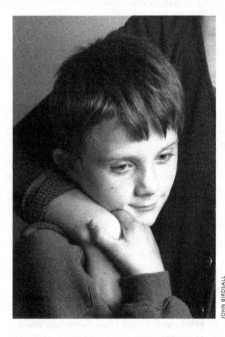

JOHN BIRDSALL

> You think that's nothing to do with
> me, but the orders are there for a
> reason. It tells you something about
> what's happened to the child and how
> concerned the social workers are about
> the kiddie's safety.
>
> Tracey, foster carer

There are different ways in which a child may come into foster care. Sometimes the parent asks for the child to be looked after; sometimes a young person approaches social services themselves; sometimes a child or young person is removed from the family because there are concerns about their welfare; and sometimes it's because a child or their carers simply need a short break. Whenever possible the move into care is planned, but on some occasions an "emergency" placement must be made.

What are the court orders which cover children coming into foster care?

In England and Wales, children often come into care on a court order made under the Children Act 1989. This may be on a temporary order, such as an emergency protection order or an interim care order. If a child is to remain in care for a long period the court may grant a care order, which lasts until the child is 18 (unless it's ended earlier by a court). Having a court order means that the local authority is able to exercise some of the "parental responsibility" that normally belongs to a family – in other words, it can make certain decisions about the child's welfare, even if the parents are not in agreement. But wherever possible, the local authority will try and work with the parent to obtain their agreement.

In Scotland, Children's Hearings make supervision requirements for children. A supervision requirement may include the child remaining in their own home, but they also cover short or long-term placements with foster carers. In an emergency, a Sheriff can make a child protection order, which means that the local authority can remove the child from their home for up to eight days. If the child remains for longer than this, the local authority needs to reapply for a warrant.

Parental responsibility orders may also be granted if children are to stay in foster care for longer periods. These orders give parental responsibility to the local authority. Section 11 (Children (Scotland) Act 1995) orders give a similar responsibility to foster carers.

> **I realised quite quickly that I needed to understand about the order the social worker had got for Suzi, when her parents just turned up on my doorstep.**
> Jenny, foster carer

Parental responsibility

Having parental responsibility for a child includes the entitlement to make all the major decisions about a child – name, education, place of residence, medical treatment, etc. Various court orders exist by which a local authority can exercise this responsibility instead of the child's parents.

As a foster carer, will I have to go to court?

You might be asked to go to court, to help the court make decisions about a child's future. The court may ask you about things the child has told you and things you have observed about the child's behaviour, or how the child's parents treat them when they visit. This will help the court to gain a clearer picture of the child's needs and to decide whether new court orders should be made, or existing ones changed or annulled.

What if the parent agrees to the child being fostered?

If parents are finding it hard to care for their child or, for example, they need to go into hospital or leave the country and have no one else to care for the child, they can ask the local authority to look after their child. This is often called "accommodation". It is covered by section 20 of the Children Act 1989 (England and Wales) and by section 25 of the Children (Scotland) Act 1995.

Because there is no court order involved and the child is placed in foster care through an agreement between the parent and the local authority, the parent can take the child home from the foster carers whenever they want. However, in Scotland, once the child has been "accommodated" for more than six months, the parent must give 14 days notice of their intention to do this.

Are there things that fostering agencies must do under the law?

Under the Children Act 1989 and the Children (Scotland) Act 1995, local authorities must comply with certain duties when they place a child with foster carers. These duties are set out in Guidance and Regulations. They cover things like the suitability of a foster placement; record keeping; visits to children in foster care; the requirements for foster carers looking after children; and things such as meetings, children's contact with families and how plans are made for children's futures. They cover the right of children and their families, and foster carers, to have access to representation and complaints procedures, if things go wrong.

I've heard about "minimum standards". What are these?

There are standards which local authorities and independent and voluntary fostering agencies must reach when they provide a fostering service. Together with the relevant fostering regulations for each country, they cover the standards of care, support and opportunities for education and personal development which must be provided for children; the responsibilities of foster carers; and the responsibilities which local authorities have for providing the service, and towards the foster carers they recruit and place children with.

As a foster carer, you will be expected to attain these minimum standards, and your agency should give you training if you need extra support in a particular area, to help you increase and develop your skills. Each year you are required to undergo an annual review when the agency has to check that you are able to continue to work to these standards. If they feel you are not able to do so, they may decide to de-register you as a carer, in accordance with the legal requirements placed on them. They will usually give you a chance to explain your reasons why you feel you should not be de-registered, and may be prepared to give you extra help to achieve the standards they require. BAAF publishes a book titled *Fostering Now*, which gives information about all the standards and regulations in England which apply to foster carers.

> **I've heard that sometimes children make allegations of abuse against their foster carers. What happens then?**

Sometimes a child or young person is very upset about something that's happening in their lives and doesn't know how to express these feelings. Or they may just feel that no one is listening to them. They may also have suffered sexual or physical abuse in the past. This may lead to children claiming that a foster carer or someone in the carer's family has physically, sexually or emotionally abused them. Many children who make such allegations later retract them, and regret that they have made them. But social workers have to take the allegations very seriously in case someone has really harmed the child or young person.

In your preparation to foster, you will learn how to provide "safe care", which makes sure that you and other members of your family don't put yourself in a situation which a vulnerable and confused child might misunderstand or misinterpret.

However, if it should happen that an allegation is made against you by a child or young person, your agency has to investigate the child's claims. Understandably this can be very upsetting, and foster care laws and guidance say that if a child makes an allegation against you or a family member, you must be treated with respect, kept properly informed about what is happening and given access to an independent person who can give you support and advice. Fostering Network has advice and mediation workers who support foster carers who are individual members of the organisation or whose fostering agency pays for these services, and some agencies provide their own mediation schemes (see Useful Organisations).

> **They came and talked to us about what he had said...we were gutted to think he could say those things...it got sorted out in the end and they said they wanted us to carry on fostering, so we said OK.**
> Steve, foster carer

What if I have a complaint?

As a foster carer, you have a right to complain if the service you receive does not meet the required standards, or if you are experiencing problems with your supervising social worker. You can also make a complaint on behalf of a child you are caring for if you have concerns about the service they are receiving. Your fostering agency will advise you of their complaints procedure.

What happens when children can't go home

JOHN BIRDSALL

> **I'm not scared any more. People here don't let me down – I feel safe and secure and well looked after and treated great. It's the best thing that could ever have happened to me.**
> 17-year-old fostered girl, *Not Just a Name*, p76

Why do some children go back to their parents and others don't?

Foster care is often used as a way of giving parents a chance to sort out their problems, so that they can take better care of their children in future. If the family is able to do this, and can show that they can care more appropriately for the child in future, the child will return home. But some families aren't able to make the adjustments to their lives that are needed to care for a child properly – even if they continue to love that child. Some children simply cannot return to their own parents because there is no home for them to go to, for example, unaccompanied refugee or asylum-seeking children. There may also be children whose parents have a serious or terminal illness, an ongoing mental health problem, or a severe learning disability, so the child cannot be cared for at home.

What happens when a child can't go home?

Even if children can't return to their own parents, they can often be cared for by someone else in the family or by someone who is a close friend of the family. If this is not possible then a family must be found who can provide "permanency" and a sense of security for the child.

There are several different ways of providing "permanency" for a child. It may be provided by long-term foster carers who care for a child until they are ready to leave care as young adults. Or the child may be adopted, if this is going to be in the best interests of the child. Children and young people are always consulted and their wishes and feelings are carefully considered when any decisions are made about their future. Older children or children who continue to have a lot of contact with their family may prefer to be long-term fostered, whereas younger children or children with little or no contact with their own families may benefit from being adopted.

> **Being part of the family taught me how society would expect me to behave as an adult. Prior to living in the family I believed that I could do what I wanted – there was no way people were going to tell me what to do.**
> Karen, *Fostering Attachments*, p 226

Parental responsibility orders and special guardianship

Foster carers may decide to apply for a residence order that allows them to take more responsibility for the care of the child. For example, in Scotland, anyone with an interest in the child's welfare – including foster carers – can apply under the provisions of section 11 of the Children (Scotland) Act 1995 for a range of parental rights, such as residence or contact. But they must be able to show that this is in the child's best interests. This order doesn't take all responsibilities and rights away from the child's own parents. It ends the local authority's formal responsibilities for the child, but the local authority may still continue to pay a residence allowance (similar to a fostering allowance). A residence order can last until the child is 18.

In England and Wales, anyone – including foster carers – can apply for a residence order if they have looked after a child for three years, or if they have the agreement of the child's parents and anyone else who has parental responsibility for the child. Someone who has looked after a child for less than three years may be allowed to apply for a residence order, but they will need to obtain the local authority's approval before the court will consider their application (unless they are relatives of the child). A residence order can be ended if someone applies to the court and the court feels there are appropriate grounds to annul it.

In England and Wales, the Adoption and Children Act 2002 has introduced a new order called special guardianship. This is intended to provide more security and permanency for children than a residence order, but without cutting the child's relationship ties with their parents. This is expected to come into force in 2005.

| Adoption

When a child is adopted, all responsibility for the child passes to the new family, as though the child had been born into that family. The local authority no longer has formal responsibility for the child, and the child's ties with their birth family are cut. Adoption is therefore a major event in a child's life, as it may mean that a child loses family ties with important people like grandparents and brothers and sisters – so it's only used where the need to provide emotional security outweighs the benefits of a child remaining part of their own family. However, many adopted children still have contact with their relatives – even if they are now legally members of a new family.

| Will I be told if the child I'm caring for can't go home?

Plans for the child's future will be explained to you when the child comes to stay with you, and you will be informed if the original plans change or develop. As a foster carer, you will be consulted and included in meetings about the child's future, so you will usually be aware of decisions that are being considered. However, many decisions are ultimately made by the courts, so there may be times when several different options are being considered for a child.

Some carers are particularly asked to care for children for whom plans for adoption are being made. If you do this type of fostering, your role is to help the child prepare for this important move in their life, and to build a good relationship with the family who will be adopting the child. Carers who do this type of work say it's very rewarding to see the joy which it brings to adoptive families – even if they feel a bit sad about saying goodbye to the child they've cared for.

What if I want to adopt a child I'm fostering?

It's important not to think of fostering as a "short cut" to adoption, and most foster care is short-term. However, there may be some children who fit particularly well into your family, and you may be able to offer this child or young person a level of care that they may not be able to receive elsewhere. For example, as the child's foster carer you will have learnt a great deal about her or his complex disabilities and emotional needs, and now feel that you are prepared to offer her or him life-time care as part of your family. Currently, about 15 per cent of children who are adopted are adopted by their foster carers, but the Adoption and Children Act 2002 (England and Wales) may increase the options for children to be adopted by foster carers.

If you decide that you want to adopt a child that you are fostering, you will need to apply to be assessed as a possible adopter. Your suitability to adopt this particular child will be considered in the same way as anyone else applying to adopt.

> ...I even remember it now and mention it to my mum now, and just laugh. And my social worker Frank came out and said, 'Well, we've made a decision but you won't know it till half past four'. Well, that was three-and-a-half hours away, then he said, 'but I can tell you now that if you'd like her to stay she can stay'. Well, that was one of the happiest days of my life. Apart from my son being born, that was. I thought 'Now I belong somewhere', because I knew them and I could get on with them.
> Woman who was fostered, in *Part of the Family*, p160

Isn't it better to adopt – because then you don't have to worry about the birth family?

Most children who are adopted these days aren't babies, and will already have developed strong emotional ties with their birth families. So most adoptions today contain an element of "openness", i.e. the child has information about their family and some contact with them, which may include meetings with family members. Even babies placed for adoption are expected to be given information about their birth families, because it's important for adopted children to know they are adopted and to have this explained to them from an early age. People who don't discover they are adopted until they are adults have said it's a very distressing experience, and often report feeling that something wasn't quite right during their childhood. Having this information available throughout childhood means that adoption becomes just another part of an adopted person's life, rather than a huge mystery that has to be solved at a later date.

The rewards of fostering

JOHN BIRDSALL

**Always remember that you can make a
real difference. It can be very
traumatic, but it can also be very
rewarding – and when you remember
that a little bit of upset for you can
change their entire life, you realise
that it really is worth it.**
Angie, foster carer, *Foster Care*, issue 113

Fostering sounds like hard work – so why do so many people do it?

People choose to foster for many reasons. Some foster carers say it's something they've wanted to do for as long as they can remember, but others find out about fostering later in life. Some people don't think about becoming foster carers until their own children or grandchildren grow up and they realise that they miss having children in their homes. Some people start to foster because their friends or family did it or they heard about it through a television or radio programme, and felt they had something special to offer.

But whatever encourages you to consider fostering in the first place, what is clear is that you really have to like children and enjoy spending time in their company. People who've fostered for a long time admit that there are some children they find easier than others, and some children aren't always easy to like, but they enjoy the satisfaction of knowing that they've made an important contribution to helping a child who is going through a very difficult time in their life.

> **I'd never have got to university if my foster mum wasn't there for me. She believed in me like no-one else did, she kept pushing the social workers and the teachers when they said it was going to be too hard for me.**
> Kayleigh, young person who was fostered

What motivates foster carers?

Again, everyone is different. But really committed foster carers tend to have one thing in common – they want to get the very best for the children and young people they're looking after. The core part of their role is providing a supportive, safe and caring environment, but committed foster carers also want to make sure that everyone else is playing their part in helping the child to get the assistance and opportunities they deserve! They'll be working closely with the school to make sure the child is receiving the extra support they need in the classroom or playground; they'll be looking for ways to develop the child's confidence and encouraging them to try new hobbies, sports and activities that boost their enjoyment and increase their self-esteem; and they'll be working closely with social workers and health professionals to make sure the child is going to the physiotherapy, speech and language development, or therapeutic sessions they need.

And carers who can see things from a child's point of view are also the ones who understand why it's important for a child to have contact with their own family. These carers recognise that children love their own parents – even if those parents have hurt them or let them down in the past. These carers accept that most children want to return home, so will do everything they can to maintain strong links between children and their own families. They may shed a few tears after a child leaves, but they'll be waving the child off cheerfully on the doorstep and genuinely wishing their family all the best for the future. And if a child can't go home, these carers will help children to remember the happy times they had with their family, as well as making sense of the sad and more painful times they experienced.

> **The satisfaction is in the small things.
> These kids may never pass any exams but
> they get a swimming certificate and
> you're so dead proud of them and all
> choked up...**
> Brenda, foster carer

What do children and young people value most from foster carers?

Young people who have been in foster care say they want carers who make time for them, listen to them and stick with them through difficult patches in their lives. They want carers who respect that they have their own family, and don't try to replace them, but who also make them feel welcome and part of their lives. They really like it when foster carers show that they believe in them and encourage them to do their best, and when they celebrate their successes and take pride in their achievements. This is important on whatever scale it may be, whether it's sitting down to eat a meal at the table for the first time, getting through a day without being sent out of the classroom, helping to organise the school play or getting good marks in an important exam.

Often looking back over their experiences in foster care, it's the seemingly small things which are the most important, and have the biggest effect on young people. They recall some little piece of advice or some practical way their foster carer helped them during a difficult time – and years later that small thing has stuck in their mind as having made a very big difference, because it showed that someone cared enough to have their interests at heart.

> **Emma comes back with her own kids now. She's got two girls and a lovely fellah who dotes on his bairns. We laugh about when she was first here – she was always packing her bags, saying she hated me and was running away...**
> Amy, foster carer

Finding a fostering agency

If you want to be considered as a foster carer, you need to apply to one of the fostering agencies in England, Scotland, Wales or Northern Ireland. Many of these are based in local authority social services departments in England and Wales, and in social work departments in Scotland. You can also apply to independent fostering agencies, which include "voluntary" agencies such as the large child care charities like Barnardo's, NCH or the Catholic Children's Society, and other independent organisations or companies which are run on a not-for-profit or profit-making basis. Some of these may have charitable status. (All independent agencies must register, are regularly inspected and must comply with the same standards as local authorities.) All of these are listed in the following pages.

In Northern Ireland, social services are provided by health and social services trusts which are commissioned by four health and social services boards. These are not listed in this book.

> **Is it best to apply to the local authority, or to an independent fostering provider or voluntary agency?**

It's best to find out what different agencies offer – and expect from you – and think about which is going to suit your circumstances and your expectations about fostering. There can be advantages and disadvantages to working with local authorities, voluntary agencies or independent fostering providers.

| Local authorities

Local authority fostering departments usually want to place children close to their own families, schools and communities, so tend to prefer applications from people within their own area. They are large organisations and have to respond to a wide range of needs, and so may not be able to offer the same level of training as some independent agencies. However, local authorities hold responsibility for all looked after children, and they will consider families they have recruited first. They will sub-contract to independent agencies to recruit more experienced families for children they have found hard to place. An increasing number of local authorities have started to run fee-paying schemes for foster carers, dependent on the level of experience of the carer, and the type of children and young people they are able to care for.

| Voluntary agencies

Voluntary agencies include large children's charities and other organisations, many of which will have charitable status. They may be looking for local foster carers, but also tend to cross local authority boundaries, so it is worth contacting agencies in counties or boroughs near to you, as well as in your own immediate area. They are often small, and specialise in fostering and adoption. They tend to offer high levels of support and training. They often specialise in foster placements for children with complex needs, and so may prefer to take on more experienced foster carers. Some voluntary agencies run fee-paying schemes for foster carers, dependent on the carer's level of experience and the type of children and young people they are able to care for.

| Independent fostering
| providers

Independent fostering providers (IFPs) will often be run on a profit-making basis but some are not and have charitable status. Like voluntary agencies, they may be looking for local foster carers, but also tend to cross local authority boundaries, so it's worth contacting IFPs in counties or boroughs near to you, as well as in your own immediate area. They tend to offer high levels of support and training. They will often specialise in foster placements for children with complex needs, and so may prefer to take on more experienced foster carers. Many independent agencies run fee-paying schemes, and may employ foster carers in the same way as any other business – paying for holiday periods when a carer has no child staying with them, and offering a fee for the work undertaken.

| What are they looking for?

All fostering agencies are looking for people who can offer high levels of care to other people's children. However, the particular needs of an agency may depend on the part of the country where they are based, or whether they have decided to specialise in certain types of fostering. For example, some local authorities and independent agencies desperately need more black and Asian carers, but in other parts of the country there are more black carers than white carers, and new white carers may be needed to provide for the needs of white children. Some local authorities and independent agencies specialise in therapeutic fostering, and they train and support foster carers to enable them to meet the needs of severely traumatised and distressed children. Or an independent fostering provider or voluntary agency may be focusing on the needs of children with disabilities, or recruiting experienced carers to foster young people remanded by the courts. You should therefore contact several agencies to find out which type of foster carers they are looking for.

| How to find a fostering
| agency

On the next few pages, you will find lists of local authorities, voluntary agencies and independent fostering providers in England, Scotland and Wales, all listed alphabetically.

When you have found the name of one or more agencies that are reasonably near you, you can phone, write or sometimes email for further information. If you are phoning, it is best to call within traditional working hours. Agencies may also have a website which you can visit. Your BAAF centre will also be able to help you (see contact details in Useful Organisations).

England: Central and Northern

Local authorities

Local authorities usually want to place children close to their own families, so tend to prefer applications from people within their area. They will be placing children with a wide range of needs, and so are likely to take on both experienced and less experienced foster carers. For more information on local authorities see p80.

BARNSLEY METROPOLITAN BOROUGH COUNCIL
Fostering and Adoption Unit
Wellington House
36 Wellington Street
BARNSLEY
S70 1WA
01226 775876
adoptionandfostering@barnsley.gov.uk

BIRMINGHAM CITY COUNCIL
The Adoption and Fostering Recruitment Team
203 Corporation Street
BIRMINGHAM
B4 6SE
0121 303 7575
a&frecruit@birmingham.gov.uk

BLACKBURN WITH DARWEN BOROUGH COUNCIL
Family Placement Team
Jubilee House
Jubilee Street
BLACKBURN
BB1 1ET
0800 328 6919

BLACKPOOL BOROUGH COUNCIL
Family Placement Team
Progress House
Clifton Road
BLACKPOOL
FY4 4US
01253 477888

BOLTON METROPOLITAN BOROUGH COUNCIL
Family Placement Unit
Woodlands
Manchester Road
BOLTON
BL3 2PQ
01204 337480

CITY OF BRADFORD METROPOLITAN COUNCIL
Adoption and Fostering Unit
35 Saltaire Road
SHIPLEY
BD18 3HH
01274 434331
adoptionfostering@bradford.gov.uk

BURY METROPOLITAN BOROUGH COUNCIL
Family Placement Team
18–20 St Marys Place
BURY
BL9 0DZ
0161 253 5457

CALDERDALE METROPOLITAN BOROUGH COUNCIL
Fostering Team
Ovenden Hall
Ovenden Road
HALIFAX
HX3 5QG
01422 353279

CHESHIRE COUNTY COUNCIL
Family Placement Support Unit
Goldsmith House
Hamilton Place
CHESTER
CH1 1SE
01244 602222
fostering@cheshire.gov.uk

COVENTRY CITY COUNCIL
Recruitment Team
Children and Families Placement Service
Stoke House
Lloyd Crescent
COVENTRY
CV2 5PY
024 766 59009
familyplacementservice@coventry.gov.uk

CUMBRIA COUNTY COUNCIL
Family Placement
Social Services
15 Portland Square
CARLISLE
CA1 1QQ
0800 169 3912

DARLINGTON COUNCIL
Fostering Team
Central House
Gladstone Street
DARLINGTON
DL3 6JX
01325 346296

DERBY CITY COUNCIL
The Fostering Team
Perth Street
Chaddesden
DERBY
DE21 6XX
01332 717723

DERBYSHIRE COUNTY COUNCIL
Fostering and Adoption Team
FREEPOST DY5
County Hall
MATLOCK
DE4 9BR
01629 772211
fostering@derbyshire.gov.uk

**DONCASTER METROPOLITAN
BOROUGH COUNCIL**
Fostering Team
PO Box 251
Council House
College Road
DONCASTER
DN1 3DA
01302 737789
social.services@doncaster.gov.uk

**DUDLEY METROPOLITAN BOROUGH
COUNCIL**
Fostering Service
Ednam House
1 St James's Road
DUDLEY
DY1 3JJ
01384 815833

DURHAM COUNTY COUNCIL
Durham Resource Centre
Fostering and Adoption
Social Care and Health
Littleburn Business Centre
Mill Road
LANGLEY MOOR
DH7 8ET
0191 370 6100
fostering@durham.gov.uk

**EAST RIDING OF YORKSHIRE
COUNCIL**
Fostering Team

31/31A Lairgate
BEVERLEY
HU17 8ET
01482 396673
do.fps@eastriding.gov.uk

**GATESHEAD METROPOLITAN
BOROUGH COUNCIL**
Fostering Team
Council Offices
Prince Consort Road
GATESHEAD
NE8 4HJ
0191 433 8333

HALTON BOROUGH COUNCIL
Adoption and Fostering Service
Grosvenor House
Halton Lea
RUNCORN
WA7 2ED
01928 704360

HARTLEPOOL BOROUGH COUNCIL
Fostering and Adoption Team
Aneurin Bevan House
35 Avenue Road
HARTLEPOOL
TS24 8HD
01429 523926

HEREFORDSHIRE COUNCIL
Children's Resource Team (Fostering)
Moor House
Widemarsh Common
HEREFORD
HR4 9NA
01432 262830

HULL CITY COUNCIL
Hull Fostering Service
Gleneagles Centre
East Carr Road

HULL
HU8 9LB
01482 798653
fostering@hullcc.gov.uk

ISLE OF MAN COUNCIL
c/o Fosterplus Ltd
11 Doolittle Mill
AMPTHILL
MK45 2ND
01525 841803
askus@fostplus.com.uk

KIRKLEES METROPOLITAN COUNCIL
Family Placement Unit
Westfields
Westfields Road
MIRFIELD
WF14 9PW
0800 389 0086
kinfo@kirklees.gov.uk

**KNOWSLEY METROPOLITAN
BOROUGH COUNCIL**
Adoption and Fostering Team
Astley House
Astley Road
HUYTON
L36 8HY
0151 443 3958

LANCASHIRE COUNTY COUNCIL
Fostering Services Manager
Social Services
East Cliff Offices
East Cliff
PRESTON
PR1 3EA
0800 195 1183
www.fosteringlancashire.co.uk

LEEDS CITY COUNCIL
Fostering and Adoption
Merrion House
LEEDS
LS2 8QB
0113 247 4747

LEICESTER CITY COUNCIL
Fostering and Adoption Centre
Eagle House
11 Friar Lane
LEICESTER
LE1 5RB
0116 299 5800
byrof001@leicester.gov.uk

LEICESTERSHIRE COUNTY COUNCIL
Family Placement Team
Bassett Street
South Wigston
LEICESTER
LE18 4PE
0116 275 9255

LINCOLNSHIRE COUNTY COUNCIL
Family Placement
Orchard House
Orchard Street
LINCOLN
LN1 1BA
0800 093 3099
fosteringandadoption@lincolnshire.gov.uk

LIVERPOOL CITY COUNCIL
Family Placement
Parklands
Customer Focus Centre
Conleach Road
LIVERPOOL
L24 0TY
0151 233 3029
*parklands.familyplacementteam@liverpool.
gov.uk*

MANCHESTER CITY COUNCIL
Family Placement Team
102 Manchester Road
Chorton-cum-Hardy
MANCHESTER
M21 9SZ
0161 881 0911
familyduty@notes.manchester.gov.uk

**MIDDLESBROUGH BOROUGH
COUNCIL**
Family Placement Team
Sandringham House
170A Overdale Road
MIDDLESBROUGH
TS3 7EA
01642 300870

**NEWCASTLE-UPON-TYNE CITY
COUNCIL**
Fostering Unit
3rd Floor
4–8 Clarence Walk
Shieldfield
NEWCASTLE-UPON-TYNE
NE2 1AL
0191 278 8359
fostering@newcastle.gov.uk

**NORTH EAST LINCOLNSHIRE
COUNCIL**
Adoption and Fostering Service
2nd Floor, St James House
St. James Square
GRIMSBY
DN31 1EP
01472 325555
fosteringandadoption@nelincs.gov.uk

NORTH LINCOLNSHIRE COUNCIL
Adoption and Fostering Team
The Grove
38 West Street

Scawby
BRIGG
DN20 9AN
01652 656005

NORTH TYNESIDE COUNCIL
Fostering Team
Camden House
Camden Street
NORTH SHIELDS
NE30 1NW
0191 200 6161
familyplacement@northtyneside.gov.uk

**NORTH YORKSHIRE COUNTY
COUNCIL**
Fostering Enquiry Centre
Jesmond House
31–33 Victoria Avenue
HARROGATE
HG1 5QG
0800 389 2362

**NORTHAMPTONSHIRE COUNTY
COUNCIL**
Fostering Services
Oxford House
West Villa Road
WELLINGBOROUGH
NN8 4JR
01604 236078
a&f@northamptonshire.gov.uk

**NORTHUMBERLAND COUNTY
COUNCIL**
Family Support and Placement Service
Tweed House
Hepscott Park
MORPETH
NE61 6NF
01670 534450

NOTTINGHAM CITY COUNCIL
Recruitment Team

York House
2nd Floor
Mansfield Road
NOTTINGHAM
NG1 3NS
0115 915 1234

**NOTTINGHAMSHIRE COUNTY
COUNCIL**
Recruitment and Publicity Team (Fostering)
20 Balderton Gate
NEWARK
NG24 1UW
0845 301 8899
fostering@nottscc.gov.uk

**OLDHAM METROPOLITAN BOROUGH
COUNCIL**
Family Placement Team
Marian Walker House
Frederick Street
OLDHAM
OL8 1SW
0161 626 4947

**REDCAR & CLEVELAND BOROUGH
COUNCIL**
Fostering Services
Grosmont Resource Centre
20 Grosmont Close
REDCAR
TS10 4PJ
01642 495918

**ROCHDALE METROPOLITAN
BOROUGH COUNCIL**
Family Placement Team
Foxholes House
Foxholes Road
ROCHDALE
OL12 0ED
01706 710750
familyplacementteam@rochdale.gov.uk

ROTHERHAM BOROUGH COUNCIL
Family Placement Service
4th Floor
Crinoline House
Effingham Square
ROTHERHAM
S65 1AW
01709 823963

RUTLAND COUNTY COUNCIL
Fostering Team
Catmose
OAKHAM
LE15 6HP
01572 758408

SALFORD CITY COUNCIL
Family Placement
Avon House
Avon Close
Salford
MANCHESTER
M28 OLA
0161 799 1762
family.placement@salford.gov.uk

**SANDWELL METROPOLITAN
BOROUGH COUNCIL**
Homefinding Team
Hollies Family Centre
Coopers Lane
SMETHWICK
B67 7DW
0121 569 5771

**SEFTON METROPOLITAN BOROUGH
COUNCIL**
Family Placement
Ellesmere House
Crosby Road North
WATERLOO
L22 0LG
0151 934 3737

*socialcare.customeraccessteam@social-
services.sefton.gov.uk*

**SHEFFIELD METROPOLITAN CITY
COUNCIL**
Family Placement Service
Floor 2
Castle Market Buildings
Exchange Street
SHEFFIELD
S1 2AH
0114 273 5075

SHROPSHIRE COUNTY COUNCIL
Fostering Resource Team
Besford House
42 Trinity Street
Belle Vue
SHREWSBURY
SY2 7PQ
0800 783 8798

**SOLIHULL METROPOLITAN
BOROUGH COUNCIL**
Fostering Team
Jubilee House
655 Auckland Drive
Smith's Wood
SOLIHULL
B36 0SN
0800 073 0769

**SOUTH TYNESIDE METROPOLITAN
BOROUGH COUNCIL**
Fostering Team
16 Barrington Street
SOUTH SHIELDS
NE33 1AN
0191 423 8500

**ST HELENS METROPOLITAN
BOROUGH COUNCIL**
Adoption and Foster Care Service

73 Corporation Street
ST HELENS
WA10 1SX
01744 456526
fostering@sthelens.gov.uk

STAFFORDSHIRE COUNTY COUNCIL
Family Placement Services
Stafford Area Office
The Business Centre
Madford Retail Park
Foregate Street
STAFFORD
ST16 2PA
0800 169 2061

**STOCKPORT METROPOLITAN
BOROUGH COUNCIL**
Fostering Team
Reddish Green Office
St Elizabeth's Way
REDDISH
SK5 6BL
0161 422 2055
familyplacement@stockport.gov.uk

**STOCKTON-ON-TEES BOROUGH
COUNCIL**
Child Placement Service
Council Offices
Town Centre
BILLINGHAM
TS23 2LW
01642 526216
child.placement@stockton.gov.uk

STOKE-ON-TRENT CITY COUNCIL
Family Placement Team
Heron Cross House
Grove Road
Fenton
STOKE-ON-TRENT
ST4 3AY

01782 234555
swann@stoke.gov.uk

SUNDERLAND CITY COUNCIL
Services for Looked After Children
Penshaw House
Station Road
Penshaw
HOUGHTON-LE-SPRING
DH4 7LB
0191 382 3108
fostering@ssd.sunderland.gov.uk

**TAMESIDE METROPOLITAN
BOROUGH COUNCIL**
Fostering Service
Union Street
HYDE
Tameside SK14 1ND
0161 368 8865

**TRAFFORD METROPOLITAN
BOROUGH COUNCIL**
Family Placement Team
4th Floor
Waterside House
Waterside
Vale
MANCHESTER
M33 7ZF
0161 912 5050
fostering@trafford.gov.uk

**WAKEFIELD METROPOLITAN
DISTRICT COUNCIL**
Family Placement Team
6 Springfield Grange
Flanshaw
WAKEFIELD
WF2 9QA
01924 302160
sc_cffamilyplace@wakefield.gov.uk

WALSALL METROPOLITAN BOROUGH COUNCIL
Duty Desk
106 Essington Rd
Essington
WILLENHALL
WV12 5DT
01922 710751

WARRINGTON BOROUGH COUNCIL
Fostering and Adoption Team
Bewsey Old School
Lockton Lane
WARRINGTON
WA5 0BF
01925 444100
fostering.adoption@warrington.gov.uk

WARWICKSHIRE COUNTY COUNCIL
Fostering Services Team
Faraday Hall
Lower Hillmorton Road
RUGBY
CV21 3TU
01926 413313
*fosteringandadoptiondevelopmentteam@
warwickshire.gov.uk*

WIGAN METROPOLITAN BOROUGH COUNCIL
Adoption and Fostering Team
Town Hall
Elliott Street
TYLDESLEY
M29 8EH
01942 404775
ssdpermanence@wiganmbc.gov.uk

WIRRAL METROPOLITAN BOROUGH COUNCIL
Duty Desk
Conway Building
Burlington Street

BIRKENHEAD
CH41 6LA
0151 666 4608

WOLVERHAMPTON CITY COUNCIL
Family Placement Service
Beldray Buildings
66 Mount Pleasant
Bilston
WOLVERHAMPTON
WV14 7PR
0800 073 0189

WORCESTERSHIRE COUNTY COUNCIL
Recruitment and Training Team (Family Placement)
Social Services Training Centre
Tolladine Road
WORCESTER
WR4 9NB
0800 028 2158

CITY OF YORK COUNCIL
Placement Services
Hollycroft
Wenlock Terrace
Fulford Road
YORK
YO10 4DU
01904 555333
adoptionandfostering@york.gov.uk

Voluntary agencies

Voluntary agencies include large children's charities and other organisations which are run on a not-for-profit basis, many of which will have charitable status. They tend to offer high levels of support and training. They will often specialise in foster placements for children with complex needs, and so may prefer to take on more experienced foster carers. Some voluntary agencies run fee-paying schemes for foster carers. For more information on voluntary agencies, see p81.

BARNARDO'S
Barnardo's runs various fostering projects. We are unable to list them all here. Please contact the address below for further details.
Tanners Lane
Barkingside
ILFORD
Essex IG5 1QG
020 8550 8822
www.barnardos.co.uk

BOYS AND GIRLS WELFARE SOCIETY
250 Wellington Road South
STOCKPORT
SK2 6NW
0161 480 8677

CHILD ACTION NORTH WEST
Whalley Road
Wilpshire
BLACKBURN
BB1 9LL
01254 248282
caresupport@canw.org.uk

CATHOLIC CARING SERVICES TO CHILDREN & COMMUNITY
2 Rodney Street
Barrow-in-Furness
CUMBRIA

LA14 3DY
01229 870349
www.catholiccaringservices.org.uk

FATHER HUDSON SOCIETY
New Routes Team
Coventry Road
Coleshill
BIRMINGHAM
B46 3EB
01675 434020
newroutes@fatherhudsons.org.uk

MANCHESTER ADOPTION SOCIETY
Goodman Team
47 Bury New Road
Sedgley Park
MANCHESTER
M25 9SY
0161 834 9916
goodman@manchesteradoption.com

ST CUTHBERTS CARE
St Cuthberts House
West Road
NEWCASTLE-UPON-TYNE
NE15 7PY
0191 228 0111
fostering@stcuthbertscare.org.uk

Independent fostering providers

Independent fostering providers (IFPs) are often run on a profit-making basis but some are not and have charitable status. They tend to offer high levels of support and training. They will often specialise in foster placements for children with complex needs, and so may prefer to take on more experienced foster carers. Many independent agencies run fee-paying schemes, and may employ foster carers in the same way as any other business. For more information on IFPs, see p 81.

ACORN FOSTERING SERVICES LTD
ASRA Conference Centre
80 Burley Way
LEICESTER
LE1 3BD
0116 251 3550

ACT IV FOSTERING AGENCY
65–67 Yardley Road
Acocks Green
BIRMINGHAM
B27 6LL
0121 707 3200

ALLIANCE FOSTER CARE
Office G2
Moulton Park Business Centre
Redhouse Road
NORTHAMPTON
NN3 6AQ
0870 240 2395
admin@alliancefostercare.co.uk

ALPHA PLUS FOSTERING SERVICES
Hollinwood Business Centre
Albert Mill
Hollinwood
OLDHAM
OL8 3QL
0161 684 2323
info@alphaplusfostering.co.uk

CARE FOSTERING SERVICES
53 Romney Street
LONDON
SW1 3RF
020 7233 0455
communications@care.org.uk

CAREFORWARD
14A Toll Gavel
BEVERLEY
HU7 9AJ
01482 864889
careforward@careforward.karoo.co.uk

CHILD CARE BUREAU
H1 Blackpole East
WORCESTER
WR3 8SG
01905 754754
childcarebureau@btconnect.com

CHILDREN'S FAMILY TRUST
MKA House
4–6 St Andrews Road
DROITWICH
WR9 8DN
01905 798229
www.thecft.org.uk

COMPASS CHILDREN'S SERVICES LTD
Desford Hall
Leicester Lane
DESFORD

LE9 9JJ
0870 850 1012
admin@compasschildren.co.uk

FIND US KEEP US
Unit 2.2
Mytton Mill
Montford Bridge
SHREWSBURY
SY4 1HA
01743 850086
finduskeepus@saccs.co.uk

FOSTER CARE ASSOCIATES EAST MIDLANDS
160 Upper New Walk
LEICESTER
LE1 7QA
0116 285 4833
0800 085 2225
www.fostercareassociates.co.uk
contactus@thefca.co.uk

FOSTER CARE ASSOCIATES MIDLANDS
Saxon View
Saxon Business Park
Hanbury Road
Stoke Prior
BROMSGROVE
B60 4AD
01527 834300
0800 085 2225
www.fostercareassociates.co.uk
contactus@thefca.co.uk

FOSTER CARE ASSOCIATES NORTH EAST
19 Portland Terrace
Jesmond
NEWCASTLE-UPON-TYNE
NE2 1QQ
0191 212 6900

0800 085 2225
www.fostercareassociates.co.uk
contactus@thefca.co.uk

FOSTER CARE ASSOCIATES NORTH WEST
Palatine House
53 Palatine Road
Withington
MANCHESTER
M20 3PP
0161 448 8228
0800 085 2225
www.fostercareassociates.co.uk
contactus@thefca.co.uk

FOSTER CARE ASSOCIATES YORKSHIRE & LINCOLNSHIRE
Ashdell Grove
60 Westbourne Road
SHEFFIELD
S10 2QU
0114 281 3363
0800 085 2225
www.fostercareassociates.co.uk
contactus@thefca.co.uk

FOSTER CARE CO-OPERATIVE
203/205 West Malvern Road
WEST MALVERN
WR14 4BB
01684 892380
enquiries@fostercarecooperative.co.uk

FOSTER CARE SERVICES NORTH WEST
65 Higher Hillgate
STOCKPORT
SK1 3HD
0161 477 0004
all@fcsnw.com

FOSTER CARE SOLUTIONS
23 Beach Road
SOUTH SHIELDS
NE33 2QA
0191 425 0095

THE FOSTERING FOUNDATION
Greengates Lodge
830A Harrogate Road
BRADFORD
BD10 0RA
01274 622622
yorks@fosteringfoundation.co.uk

FOSTERING PEOPLE LTD
St Clement's House
61 Trent Boulevard
West Bridgford
NOTTINGHAM
NG2 5BE
0115 914 5301
info@fosteringpeople.co.uk

FOSTERING SOLUTIONS
15 Chorley Old Road
BOLTON
BL1 3AD
0845 230 5505
enquiries@fosteringsolutions.com

FREEDOM FOSTERING
Suite 19/20
Saturn Facilities
Spring Road
Ettingshall
WOLVERHAMPTON
WV4 6JX
01902 491140
blenheimservices@bt.com

INDEPENDENT FOSTERING LTD
3 Clarence Street
NOTTINGHAM

NG3 2ET
0115 947 3328
placements@independentfostering.co.uk

JAY FOSTERING LTD
Unit I
Edward House
Grange Business Park
Whetstone
LEICESTER
LE8 6EP
0116 277 0066
enquiries@jfostering.co.uk

**JIGSAW (NORTH WEST) INDEPENDENT
FOSTERING AGENCY LTD**
The Old Courthouse
Chapel Street
DUKINFIELD
SK16 4DT
0161 609 1282
theteam@jigsaw-nw.org.uk

LORIMER FOSTER SERVICES
Lorimer House
2A Carrington Lane
Sale
MANCHESTER
M33 5ND
08701 203520

**ORANGE GROVE FOSTER CARE
AGENCY**
Orange Grove House
Upper Interfields
Leigh Sinton Road
MALVERN
WR14 1UT
01886 833860
enquiries@theorangegrove.co.uk

PARALLEL PARENTS (CARE TODAY)
Suite 6, New Mansion House
173–191 Wellington Road South
STOCKPORT
Cheshire SK1 3UA
0161 477 5830

PREMIER FOSTER CARE LTD
24 The Square
Dobcross
SADDLEWORTH
OL3 5AA
01457 829400
admin@premierfostercare.org.uk

PROGRESS CHILDREN'S SERVICES
Progress House
127 Millfields Road
WOLVERHAMPTON
WV4 6JG
01902 561066
mail@progresschildrensservices.co.uk

REACH-OUT CARE LTD
26 Longfield Road
Wear Valley Business Centre
Innovation House
South Church
BISHOP AUCKLAND
DL14 6XB
0191 383 0847

SOLUTIONS FOSTERING AGENCY
The Business Centre
Llangarron
ROSS-ON-WYE
HR9 6PG
01989 770770

SURECARE365
6 George Street
Cottingham
HULL
HU16 5QU
01482 846650
info@surecare365.co.uk

SWIIS FOSTER CARE
Victoria Square House
81 New Street
BIRMINGHAM
B2 4BA
0121 643 4609

TEAM FOSTERING
Howden Terminal
Willington Quay
WALLSEND
NE28 6UL
0191 262 8855
info@teamfostering.co.uk

England: Southern

Local authorities

Local authorities usually want to place children close to their own families, so tend to prefer applications from people within their area. They will be placing children with a wide range of needs, and so are likely to take on both experienced and less experienced foster carers. For more information on local authorities see p 80.

For London boroughs, please see the end of this section.

**BATH AND NORTH EAST SOMERSET
COUNCIL**
Family Placement Team
Social and Housing Services
PO Box 3373
BATH
BA1 2ZH
01225 394949

BEDFORDSHIRE COUNTY COUNCIL
Family Placement
Houghton Lodge
Houghton Close, off Oliver Street
AMPTHILL
MK45 2TG
01525 631043
fpduty@bedscc.gov.uk

BOURNEMOUTH BOROUGH COUNCIL
Duty Desk
Placements Team
27 Slades Farm Road
Ensbury Park
BOURNEMOUTH
BH10 4ES
01202 456718
fostering@bournemouth.gov.uk

**BRACKNELL FOREST BOROUGH
COUNCIL**
Family Placement Team
Social Services and Housing

Time Square
Market Street
BRACKNELL
RG12 1JD
01344 351557
family.placement@bracknell-forest.gov.uk

BRIGHTON AND HOVE COUNCIL
Fostering Team
253 Preston Road
BRIGHTON
BN1 6SE
01273 295444
fosteringandadoption@brighton-hove.gov.uk

BRISTOL CITY COUNCIL
Family Placement Team
Avonvale Road
Redfield
BRISTOL
BS5 9RH
0117 954 8546

**BUCKINGHAMSHIRE COUNTY
COUNCIL**
Fostering and Adoption
County Hall
Walton Street
AYLESBURY
HP20 1UA
01296 382555
fostering@buckscc.gov.uk

CAMBRIDGESHIRE COUNTY COUNCIL
Fostering and Adoption
Buttsgrove Centre
38 Buttsgrove Way
HUNTINGDON
PE29 1LY
0800 052 0078
fanda@cambridgeshire.gov.uk

CORNWALL COUNTY COUNCIL
Foster Care Service
County Hall
TRURO
TR1 3AY
01872 323638

CROYDON SOCIAL SERVICES DEPARTMENT
Fostering Recruitment and Assessment Team
Fostering and Adoption Services
Taberner House
Park Lane
CROYDON
CR9 2BA
020 8686 4433

DEVON COUNTY COUNCIL
Fostering Team
Magdalen House
56 Magdalen Road
EXETER
EX2 4TL
01392 384942
info@devon.gov.uk

DORSET COUNTY COUNCIL (EAST)
Adoption and Fostering Unit
Pippins
Hanham Road
WIMBOURNE
BH21 1AS
01202 889969

DORSET COUNTY COUNCIL (WEST)
Adoption and Fostering Team
Dorset County Council Social Care and Health
Acland Road
DORCESTER
DT1 1SH
01305 251414
socialcare@dorsetcc.gov.uk

EAST SUSSEX COUNTY COUNCIL
Fostering Team
6th Floor
St Marys House
5 St Leonards Road
EASTBOURNE
BN21 3UU
01323 747499
fostering@eastsussex.gov.uk

ESSEX COUNTY COUNCIL
Adoption and Fostering Recruitment
125–127 New London Road
CHELMSFORD
CM2 0QT
0800 801530
adoptionandfostering@essex.gov.uk

GLOUCESTERSHIRE COUNTY COUNCIL
Fostering Team
Social Services Department
39–41 London Road
CHELTENHAM
GL52 6XJ
01242 532654
fostering@gloucestershire.gov.uk

GUERNSEY, STATES OF
Department of Health and Social Services
Home Finding Services
Garden Hill Resource Centre
Rohais
St Peter Port

GUERNSEY
GY1 1FB
01481 713230

HAMPSHIRE COUNTY COUNCIL
County Fostering Services
Glen House
Glen Road
Swanwick
SOUTHAMPTON
SO31 7HD
0845 601 1895
www.hants.gov.uk/fostering

HERTFORDSHIRE COUNTY COUNCIL
0800 9170 925

ISLE OF WIGHT COUNTY COUNCIL
Family Placement Team
Ryde Neighbourhood Office
Ryde Town Hall
Lind Street
RYDE
PO33 2NQ
01983 566011

STATES OF JERSEY
Fostering Enquiries
Social Services
Maison Le Pape
The Parade
ST HELIER
JE2 3PU
01534 623500

KENT COUNTY COUNCIL
Fostering Initial Enquiries Team
17 Kings Hill Avenue
WEST MALLING
ME19 4UL
0845 330 2968
www.kentfostering.com

MEDWAY COUNCIL
Homefinding Team
Compass Centre
Chatham Maritime
CHATHAM
ME4 4YH
01634 306000

MILTON KEYNES COUNCIL
Fostering Services
Saxon Court
502 Avebury Boulevard
CENTRAL MILTON KEYNES
MK9 3HS
01908 253206

NORFOLK COUNTY COUNCIL
Recruitment and Assessment Team
Grove Lane
HOLT
NR25 6ED
0800 005007
fostering@norfolk.gov.uk

**NORTH SOMERSET DISTRICT
COUNCIL**
Adoption and Fostering Team
PO Box 195
Town Hall
WESTON-SUPER-MARE
BS23 1UF
01275 888 999
fostering@n_somerset.gov.uk

OXFORDSHIRE COUNTY COUNCIL
City Family Placement Team
134B Cowley Road
OXFORD
OX4 1JH
01865 375515
shc@oxfordshire.gov.uk

PETERBOROUGH CITY COUNCIL
Adoption and Fostering Team
Suite 6
Staniland Court
Staniland Way
Werrington
PETERBOROUGH
PE4 6NJ
0800 085 0713
afuduty@peterborough.gov.uk

PLYMOUTH CITY COUNCIL
Family Placement Team
Midland House
Notte Street
PLYMOUTH
PL1 2AA
01752 306805

POOLE BOROUGH COUNCIL
Adoption and Fostering Team
14A Commercial Road
Parkstone
POOLE
BH14 OJW
01202 714711

PORTSMOUTH CITY COUNCIL
Family Placement Team
12 Chaucer House
Isambard Brunel Road
PORTSMOUTH
PO1 2EP
023 9282 9846
fostering@portsmouthcc.gov.uk

READING BOROUGH COUNCIL
Fostering and Adoption Team
PO Box 2624
READING
RG1 7WB
01189 553740

SLOUGH BOROUGH COUNCIL
Family Placement Service
Town Hall
Bath Road
SLOUGH
SL1 3UQ
0800 073 0291
familyplacement@slough.gov.uk

SOMERSET COUNTY COUNCIL
Recruitment Co-ordinator
Fostering and Adoption
PO Box 29
ILMINSTER
TA19 9YG
0800 587 9900

SOUTH GLOUCESTERSHIRE COUNCIL
Family Placement Team
Heath Resource Centre
2A Newton Road
CADBURY HEATH
BS30 8EZ
01454 868222

SOUTHAMPTON CITY COUNCIL
Foster Care Service
315 Coxford Road
SOUTHAMPTON
SO16 5LH
023 8079 9242

SOUTHEND COUNCIL
Family Finders
283 London Road
WESTCLIFF-ON-SEA
SS0 7BX
01702 354366

SUFFOLK COUNTY COUNCIL
Fostering and Link Team
Shire Hall
BURY ST EDMUNDS

IP33 1RX
0800 328 2148
fostering@socserv.suffolkcc.gov.uk

SURREY COUNTY COUNCIL
Family Finding and Recruitment Team
Freepost KT2458
The Meads
CHERTSEY
KT15 2EP
0800 0969 626
fostering@surreycc.gov.uk

SWINDON BOROUGH COUNCIL
Family Placement Team
Hut 8, Civic Offices
Euclid Street
SWINDON
SN1 2JH
01793 465700
familyplacement@swindon.gov.uk

THURROCK COUNCIL
Family Placement Team Civic Offices
New Road
GRAYS
RM17 6TJ
01375 652620
information@thurrockfostering.gov.uk

TORBAY COUNCIL
Foster Care Service
Parkfield House
38 Esplanade Road
PAIGNTON
TQ3 7NH
01803 402781

WEST BERKSHIRE COUNCIL
Family Placement Team
1st Floor
Avonbank House

West Street
NEWBURY
RG14 1BZ
01635 503155

WEST SUSSEX COUNTY COUNCIL
Family Placement Service
Harwood House
Kings Road
HORSHAM
RH13 5PR
01403 246400
family.placement.north@westsussex.gov.uk

WILTSHIRE COUNTY COUNCIL
Family Placement Team
Riverside Children's Resource Centre
29 Church Fields Road
SALISBURY
SP2 7NH
0800 169 6321

ROYAL BOROUGH OF WINDSOR &
MAIDENHEAD
Fostering, Adoption and Respite Services
Social Services Directorate
Maidenhead Office
4 Marlow Road
MAIDENHEAD
SL6 7YR
01628 683201
adoption&fostering@rbwm.gov.uk

WOKINGHAM DISTRICT COUNCIL
Family Placement Team
Lytham Court
Lytham Road
WOODLEY
RG5 3PQ
0118 944 5468
familyplacement@wokingham.gov.uk

London boroughs

LONDON BOROUGH OF BARKING & DAGENHAM
Fostering Team
512A Heathway
DAGENHAM
RM10 7SL
020 8227 5822
fostering@barking-dagenham.gov.uk

LONDON BOROUGH OF BARNET
Family Placement Team
Barnet House, 6th Floor
1255 High Road
Whetstone
LONDON
N20 0EJ
0800 389 8740

LONDON BOROUGH OF BEXLEY
Children's Placement Service
Howbury Centre
Slade Green Road
ERITH
DA8 2HX
020 8303 7777 ext. 3831/3845
adoption&fostering@bexley.gov.uk

LONDON BOROUGH OF BRENT
Placements Service
Triangle House
328–330 High Road
WEMBLEY
HA9 6AZ
020 8937 4559/4519

LONDON BOROUGH OF BROMLEY
Fostering and Adoption Information
PO Box 381
BROMLEY
BR2 0ZX
0800 028 8298
fostering&adoption@bromley.gov.uk

LONDON BOROUGH OF CAMDEN
Fostering Team
115 Wellesley Road
LONDON
NW5 4PA
020 7974 1270

LONDON BOROUGH OF EALING
Children's Placement Service
2nd Floor
Acton Town Hall
Winchester Street
LONDON
W3 6NE
0800 731 6550
fosteradopt@ealing.gov.uk

LONDON BOROUGH OF ENFIELD
Fostering and Adoption Team
Looked After Children
Southgate Town Hall
Green Lanes
Palmers Green
LONDON
N13 4XD
020 8379 2809

LONDON BOROUGH OF GREENWICH
Fostering Services
Recruitment, Assessment and Monitoring
Team
147 Powis Street
Woolwich
LONDON
SE18 6JL
0800 052 1499
fostering@greenwich.gov.uk

LONDON BOROUGH OF HACKNEY
Hackney Fostering
205 Morning Lane
LONDON
E9 6JX

0800 0730 418
www.hackneykids.org.uk

**LONDON BOROUGH OF
HAMMERSMITH & FULHAM**
Family Placement Unit
2nd Floor
Barclay House
Effie Road
LONDON
SW6 1EN
0800 169 3497

LONDON BOROUGH OF HARINGEY
Adoption and Fostering
4th Floor
40 Cumberland Road
Wood Green
LONDON
N22 7SG
020 8489 3754
fostering.adoption@haringey.gov.uk

LONDON BOROUGH OF HARROW
Family Placement
429–433 Pinner Road
NORTH HARROW
HA1 4HN
020 8728 8871
fpuduty@harrow.gov.uk

LONDON BOROUGH OF HAVERING
Family Placement Service
Midland House
109–113 Victoria Road
ROMFORD
RM7 2LX
01708 434576

LONDON BOROUGH OF HILLINGDON
Fostering and Adoption Service
855 Uxbridge Road
HAYES

UB4 8HZ
01895 277 850
placementservice@hillingdon.gov.uk

LONDON BOROUGH OF HOUNSLOW
Family Placement Section
Pavillion BF
Lampton Road
LONDON
TW3 4DN
0800 731 8558
fosteringinfo.sshp@hounslow.gov.uk

LONDON BOROUGH OF ISLINGTON
Islington Fostering Service
292 Essex Road
LONDON
N1 3AZ
0800 073 0428
fostering@islington.gov.uk

**ROYAL BOROUGH OF KENSINGTON &
CHELSEA**
Fostering Team
Westway Information Centre
140 Ladbroke Grove
LONDON
W10 5ND
020 7598 4499
adopt-fosterus@rbkc.gov.uk

**LONDON BOROUGH OF KINGSTON-
UPON-THAMES**
Family Placement Team
Room 205
Guildhall
KINGSTON-UPON-THAMES
KT1 1EU
020 8547 6042
famplacduty@rbk.kingston.gov.uk

LONDON BOROUGH OF LAMBETH

Fostering and Adoption
Mary Seacole House
91 Clapham High Street
LONDON
SW4 7TF
0800 952 2926

LONDON BOROUGH OF LEWISHAM

Fostering Team
1st Floor
Laurence House
1 Catford Road
LONDON
SE6 4RU
020 8314 6655

CORPORATION OF LONDON

Department of Community Services
Children and Families Team
PO Box 270
Guildhall
LONDON
EC2P 2EJ
020 7332 1224

LONDON BOROUGH OF LUTON

Fostering Services Team
Unity House
111 Stuart Street
LUTON
LU1 5NP
01582 547737
fosteringteam@luton.gov.uk

LONDON BOROUGH OF MERTON

Fostering Team
Worsfold House
Church Road
MITCHAM
CR4 3BE
0800 073 0874
fostering@merton.gov.uk

LONDON BOROUGH OF NEWHAM

Placement Services
16 Wordsworth Avenue
Manor Park
LONDON
E12 6SU
0800 013 0393
ffd-pams@newham.gov.uk

LONDON BOROUGH OF REDBRIDGE

Fostering and Adoption Service
Station Road
BARKINGSIDE
IG6 1NB
020 8708 7460

**LONDON BOROUGH OF RICHMOND-
UPON-THAMES**

Fostering Team
42 York Street
TWICKENHAM
TW1 3BW
0800 085 7072

LONDON BOROUGH OF SOUTHWARK

Adoption and Fostering Unit
47B East Dulwich Road
LONDON
SE22 9BZ
020 7525 1199

LONDON BOROUGH OF SUTTON

Adoption and Fostering Team
The Lodge
Honeywood Walk
CARSHALTON
SM5 3NX
020 8770 4250
info@suttonfostering.org.uk

LONDON BOROUGH OF TOWER HAMLETS
Family Placement Service
Woodstock Terrace
117 Poplar High Street
LONDON
E14 0AE
0800 279 9850
fostering@towerhamlets.gov.uk

LONDON BOROUGH OF WALTHAM FOREST
Fostering and Adoption Service
1C The Drive
LONDON
E17 3BN
020 8496 2479

LONDON BOROUGH OF WANDSWORTH
Adoption and Fostering
Welbeck House
43–51 Wandsworth High Street
LONDON
SW18 2PU
020 8871 6666
adoptionandfostering@wandsworth.gov.uk

WESTMINSTER CITY COUNCIL
Family Placement
Westminster City Council
33 Tachbrook Street
LONDON
SW1V 2JR
020 7641 6304

Voluntary agencies

Voluntary agencies include large children's charities and other organisations which are run on a not-for-profit basis, many of which will have charitable status. They tend to offer high levels of support and training. They will often specialise in foster placements for children with complex needs, and so may prefer to take on more experienced foster carers. Some voluntary agencies run fee-paying schemes for foster carers. For more information on voluntary agencies, see p81.

BARNARDO'S
Barnardo's runs various fostering projects. We are unable to list them all here. Please contact the address below for further details.
Tanners Lane
Barkingside
ILFORD
IG5 1QG
020 8550 8822
www.barnardos.co.uk

CATHOLIC CHILDREN'S SOCIETY
Foster Care Service
7A Bridge Street
WINCHESTER

SO23 0HN
0800 389 9041; 01962 854652
fosterwinchester@cathchild.org

CORAM FAMILY
Adoption and Permanent Family Service
49 Mecklenburgh Square
LONDON
WC1N 2QA
020 7520 0383
adoption@coram.org.uk

NCH
Family Placement Services
158 Crawley Road, Roffey

HORSHAM
RH12 4EU
01403 225900
www.nch.org.uk/fostercare

**NORWOOD FOSTERING AND
ADOPTION SERVICES**
Broadway House
80–82 The Broadway
STANMORE
HA7 4HB
020 8954 4554
sara.lurie@norwood.org.uk

**PARENTS AND CHILDREN TOGETHER
(PACT)**
7 Southern Court, South Street
READING
RG1 4QS
0118 938 7600
info@pactcharity.org

PARENTS FOR CHILDREN
Club Union House
253–254 Upper Street
LONDON
N1 1RY
020 7288 4320
fostering@parentsforchildren.co.uk

Independent fostering providers

Independent fostering providers (IFPs) will often be run on a profit-making basis, but some are not and have charitable status. They tend to offer high levels of support and training. They will often specialise in foster placements for children with complex needs, and so may prefer to take on more experienced foster carers. Many independent agencies run fee-paying schemes, and may employ foster carers in the same way as any other business. For more information on IFPs, see p81.

ADVANCE FOSTER CARE LTD
13 Oakmount Road
Chandlers Ford
EASTLEIGH
SO53 2LG
023 8025 8500
info@advancefostercare.com

ARCHWAY CARE LTD
Hounslow Hall Estate
NEWTON LONGVILLE
MK17 0BU
01908 379400

ASPHALEIA LTD
9 Liverpool Terrace
WORTHING
BN11 1TA

01903 522966
contactus@asphaleia.co.uk

**ASSOCIATED FOSTERCARE
SERVICES**
5 Cecil Square
MARGATE
CT9 1BD
01843 229522
afs@margate46.freeserve.co.uk

**BANYA FAMILY PLACEMENT
AGENCY**
Croxted Mews
Unit 6
286A–288 Croxted Mews
Croxted Road
LONDON

SE24 9DA
020 8678 5330
info@banyanet.com

BY THE BRIDGE LTD
The Oast House
Wrens Road
Borden
SITTINGBOURNE
ME9 8JE
0845 450 9944

CHILDREN FIRST FOSTERING
AGENCY LTD
2nd Floor
Warren House
10–20 Main Road
HOCKLEY
SS5 4QS
01702 208520
children-first@cffa.co.uk

CHILDREN OF COLOUR LTD
83 Mayow Road
LONDON
SE26 4AA
020 8699 9010
childrenofcolour@aol.com

CHILDREN UNITE FOSTERCARE
75 Trinity Road
Tooting Bec
LONDON
SW17 7SQ
020 8767 6430
info@childrenunitefostercare.co.uk

CHRYSALIS CARE
51 Highfield Road
DARTFORD
DA1 2JS
0845 230 6656
chrysaliscare@yahoo.com

COMMUNITY FOSTER CARE
Twigworth Court Business Centre
Tewkesbury Road
Twigworth
GLOUCESTER
GL2 9PG
01452 731144
info@communityfostercare.co.uk

CORNERWAYS FOSTERING SERVICES
Lyttel Hall
Coopers Hill Road
NUTFIELD
RH1 4HY
01737 824290
fostering@cornerways.org

CREDO CARE LTD
PO Box 29
ROMNEY MARSH
TN29 9ZN
0870 241 4285
enquiries@credocare.co.uk

CROHAM CARE SERVICES
45 Croham Road
SOUTH CROYDON
CR2 7HD
020 8406 5300
fostering@croham.co.uk

EAST LONDON FOSTER CARERS
2A Thorpe Road
East Ham
LONDON
E6 2HS
020 8470 2088
admin@elfcarers.org.uk

ELITE FOSTERING LTD
37 Western Road
MITCHAM
CR4 3ED

020 8648 5378
elitefostering@btconnect.com

ETHELBERT RESIDENTIAL FAMILY
PLACEMENTS LTD
The Lodge
Eastry
SANDWICH
CT13 0NY
01304 621619
enquiries@ethelbertfamilyplacements.co.uk

FAMILIES FIRST (SW) LLP
8A Powderham Road
NEWTON ABBOT
TQ12 1EU
01626 333787
familiesfirst@eclipse.co.uk

FAMILIES FOR CHILDREN
1st Floor
6–7 Lovers Walk
BRIGHTON
BN1 6AH
01273 543700
resources@families-for-children.co.uk

FAMILY MATTERS FOSTERING LTD
127 Sandgate Road
FOLKESTONE
CT20 2BL
01303 210029
enquiries@fml.org.uk

FIRST POINT FOSTERING LTD
Unit 2
Vanguard Business Centre
Alperton Lane
GREENFORD
UB6 8AA
020 8206 1066
fpfostering@aol.com

FIVE RIVERS FAMILY PLACEMENT
SERVICE
Belmont School
School Lane
SALISBURY
SP1 3YA
01722 421142
neil.loader@five-rivers.org

FOREST CARE FOSTERING SERVICES
LTD
Waltham Forest Business Centre
5 Blackhorse Lane
LONDON
E17 6DS
020 8531 5556
careforest@hotmail.com

FOSTER CARE ASSOCIATES EAST
ANGLIA
Sorrel House
Claydon Business Park
Dipping Road
Great Blakenham
IPSWICH
IP6 0NL
01473 833998
0800 085 2225
www.fostercareassociates.co.uk
contactus@thefca.co.uk

FOSTER CARE ASSOCIATES KENT
Unit 1
New Court
1 New Road
ROCHESTER
ME1 1BD
01634 842777
0800 085 2225
www.fostercareassociates.co.uk
contactus@thefca.co.uk

FOSTER CARE ASSOCIATES LONDON
150–154 Borough High Street
LONDON
SE1 1LB
020 74032856
0800 085 2225
www.fostercareassociates.co.uk
contactus@thefca.co.uk

FOSTER CARE ASSOCIATES SOLENT
21 Cumberland Place
SOUTHAMPTON
SO15 2BB
023 8063 8020
0800 085 2225
www.fostercareassociates.co.uk
contactus@thefca.co.uk

FOSTER CARE ASSOCIATES SOUTH EAST
Unit 10
Britannia Business Park
Comet Way
SOUTHEND-ON-SEA
SS2 6GE
01702 421155
0800 085 2225
www.fostercareassociates.co.uk
contactus@thefca.co.uk

FOSTER CARE ASSOCIATES SOUTH WEST
Ground Floor
Lyster Court
The Millfields
PLYMOUTH
PL1 3JB
01752 254554
0800 085 2225
www.fostercareassociates.co.uk
contactus@thefca.co.uk

FOSTER CARE ASSOCIATES THAMES VALLEY
The Cottages
57–65 The Broadway
STANMORE
HA7 4DJ
020 8954 6254
0800 085 2225
www.fostercareassociates.co.uk
contactus@thefca.co.uk

FOSTER CARE ASSOCIATES WESTERN
13 Whiteladies Road
Clifton
BRISTOL
BS8 1PB
0117 9238383
0800 085 2225
www.fostercareassociates.co.uk
contactus@thefca.co.uk

FOSTER CARE LINK (ISLAMIC FOSTERING SERVICE)
159B Stoke Newington High Street
LONDON
N16 0NY
020 7923 0330
admin@fostercarelink.com

THE FOSTERING FOUNDATION LTD (LONDON)
122 Cranbrook Road
ILFORD
IG1 4LZ
020 8518 1177
london@fosteringfoundation.co.uk

THE FOSTERING FOUNDATION LTD (WESSEX)
The Old Fire Station
Christchurch Street West
FROME
BA11 1EH

01373 473 383
mail@fosteringfoundation.co.uk

FOSTERING OPTIONS LTD
Threshing House
Hayfield Business Park
Aspley Guise
MILTON KEYNES
MK17 8HS
01908 587666
services@fostering-options.org

FOSTERPLUS LTD
11 Doolittle Mill
Froghall Road
AMPTHILL
MK45 2ND
01525 841803
askus@fosterplus.co.uk

FUTURES FOR CHILDREN
69 College Road
MAIDSTONE
ME15 6SX
0870 224 9031

GLOBAL FOSTERING LTD
62 New Church Road
LONDON
SE5 7JP
020 7703 2585

GREATER LONDON FOSTERING LTD
Interiors House
Lynton Road
LONDON
N8 8SL
020 8347 8741
info@greaterlondonfostering.org

HAPPEN FOSTERCARE LTD
6 West Bar Street

BANBURY
OX16 9RR
01295 271103
admin@happenfostercare.co.uk

HARBOUR FOSTER FAMILIES
Temple Grove
Compton Place Road
EASTBOURNE
BN20 8AD
01323 749767
harbour@hff.org.uk

HEATH FARM FAMILY SERVICES
Heath Farm
Charing Heath
ASHFORD
TN27 OAX
01233 712030
dthirlaway@heathfarm.co.uk

HILLCREST FOSTER CARE LTD
Millfield
HIGH HALDEN
TN26 3LX
01233 850060
hillcrestfoster@btconnect.com

THE HOMEFINDING AND FOSTERING AGENCY LTD
67 College Road
MAIDSTONE
ME15 6SX
01622 765646
kent@homefinding.fsnet.co.uk

HORIZON FOSTERING SERVICES LTD
Kingsbury House
468 Church Lane
LONDON
NW9 8UA
020 8200 2355
info@horizonfostering.co.uk

INDEPENDENT ASIAN FOSTERING BUREAU
Suite 2, 2nd Floor
South Park Business Centre
310 Green Lane
ILFORD
IG1 1XT
020 8597 8458
www.iafb.co.uk

INTEGRATED SERVICES PROGRAMME
Central Office
Church Street
SITTINGBOURNE
ME10 3EG
01795 428097
enquiries@ispchildcare.org.uk

KALEIDOSCOPE
Keystun
Ruins Barn Road
Tunstall
nr SITTINGBOURNE
ME9 8AA
01795 830006
admin@kaleidoscope-fostercare.co.uk

KASPER
107B Island Wall
WHITSTABLE
CT5 1EL
01227 275985
mail@kasperfostering.org

KINDERCARE FOSTERING LTD
Kelsey House
77 High Street
BECKENHAM
BR3 1AN
020 8663 6327
info@kindercare.co.uk

MALVERN GRANGE FOSTER CARE
15 Warwick Road
Cliftonville
MARGATE
CT9 2JU
01843 223555

MOMENTS PROFESSIONAL FOSTERING AGENCY
Holme Lodge Farm
Pean Hill
WHITSTABLE
CT5 3AY
01227 479444
www.momentspfa.plus.com

MUSLIM FOSTERING SOCIETY UK
Units 20–23
Wilmer Industrial Estate
Wilmer Place
Stoke Newington
LONDON
N16 0LW
020 7923 3333
info@muslimfostering.co.uk

NATIONAL FOSTERING AGENCY
Uxbridge House
464 Uxbridge Road
HAYES
UB4 0SP
020 8848 7878

NENE VALLEY FOSTERING AGENCY
12B Market Place
Oundle
PETERBOROUGH
PE8 4BQ
01832 274715
nvfaenquiry@aol.com

NEXT STEP FOSTERING
Leslie Ward

Wren's Hill House
Rushett Lane
Norton
FAVERSHAM
ME13 0SH
01795 521739
info@nextstepfostering.org

NEXUS FOSTERING
Temple House
221–225 Station Road
HARROW
HA1 2TH
020 8861 8330
info@nexusfostering.co.uk

OUTLOOK FOSTERING SERVICES LTD
2 Willow House
32 Kennington Road
Willesborough
ASHFORD
TN24 0NR
01233 610661
fostering@outlookltd.com

PARTNERS IN PARENTING LTD
Cambridge House
91 High Street
LONGSTANTON
CB4 5BS
01954 781642
enquiries@partnersinparenting.org.uk

**PRO-TEEN FAMILY PLACEMENT
SERVICE**
Suite 1, 1 Chaucer House
Watery Lane
Kemsing
SEVENOAKS
TN15 6PL
01732 763763
ross.proteenltd@btconnect.com

QUALITY FOSTER CARE LTD
305A High Road
BENFLEET
SS7 5HA
01268 795597
admin@qualityfostercare.com

RURAL FOSTERCARE LTD
Teignbridge Business Centre
Cavalier Road
Heathfield
NEWTON ABBOT
TQ12 6TZ
01626 835060
ruralfostercare@teignbc.fsnet.co.uk

RYANCARE FOSTERING LTD
Oak House
5A Wellington Road
LONDON
E11 2AN
020 8989 4970
ryancare@btopenworld.com

SAFE HAVEN CONSULTANCY LTD
37 Davids Road
Forest Hill
LONDON
SE23 3EP
020 8699 1771
safehaven_consultancy@virgin.net

SAFEHOUSES
Pippa's End Wood Farm
Burlings Lane
Knockholt
SEVENOAKS
TN14 7PF
01959 534000

SEAFIELDS FOSTERING LTD
29–31 Malvern Road
HORNCHURCH

RM11 1BG
01708 733735

SEDGEMOOR
Ashwell Park
ILMINSTER
TA19 9DX
01460 258000

STIMSON HOUSE SERVICES LTD
Stimson House
1–19 Eastern Esplanade
CLIFTONVILLE
CT9 2HH
01843 224324
headoffice@stimsonhouse.co.uk

SUNBEAM FOSTERING AGENCY LTD
Research House
Fraser Road
Perivale
MIDDLESEX
UB6 7AQ
020 8537 3480/1
sunbeamfostering@aol.com

SUPPORTED FOSTERING SERVICES
CHARITABLE TRUST
26 The Hill
NORTHFLEET
DA11 9EU
01474 365500
kent@fostering.com

SYNERGY FOSTERING
2nd Floor
Barkat House
116–118 Finchley Road
LONDON
NW3 5HT
020 7433 2545
enquiries@synergy-fostering.co.uk

THE ADOLESCENT CHILDREN'S
TRUST (TACT)
The Courtyard
303 Hither Green Lane
LONDON
SE13 6TJ
020 8695 8142
www.tact-fostercare.org.uk

VISION FOSTERING AGENCY LTD
Bridge House
High Street
DARTFORD
DA1 1DJ
01322 629260
enquiries@visiongroup.uk.com

VITALITY FOSTERING AGENCY
Unit 9
293 Luton Road
DUNSTABLE
LU5 4PR
01582 676353

WOODSIDE FOSTERCARE LTD
7 Nelson Street
STROUD
GL5 2HL
01453 759836
admin@woodsidefostercare.co.uk

THE XCEL 2000 PARTNERSHIP LTD
8 London Road
SITTINGBOURNE
ME10 1NA
01795 470222
enquiries@xcel2000.com

Scotland

Local authorities

Local authorities usually want to place children close to their own families, so tend to prefer applications from people within their area. They will be placing children with a wide range of needs, and so are likely to take on both experienced and less experienced foster carers. For more information on local authorities, see page 80.

CITY OF ABERDEEN COUNCIL
Fostering and Adoption Services
77/79 King Street
ABERDEEN
AB24 5AB
01224 793830

ABERDEENSHIRE COUNCIL
Family Placement Team
93 High Street
INVERURIE
AB51 3AB
01467 625555

ANGUS COUNCIL
Family Placement Team
Academy Lane
ARBROATH
DD11 1EJ
01241 435078

ARGYLL AND BUTE COUNCIL
Family Placement Team
13A East King Street
HELENSBURGH
G84 7QQ
01436 677186

CLACKMANNANSHIRE COUNCIL
Family Placement Team
Alloa Centre, 8 Hillcrest Drive
ALLOA
FK10 1SB
01259 225000

DUMFRIES AND GALLOWAY COUNCIL
Fostering and Adoption Team
27 Moffat Road
DUMFRIES
DG1 1NB
01387 260677

DUNDEE CITY COUNCIL
Family Placement Team
6 Kirkton Road
DUNDEE
DD3 0BZ
01382 436060
reception.kirkton@dundeecity.gov.uk

EAST AYRSHIRE COUNCIL
Children and Families (Fostering)
Civic Centre
John Dickie Street
KILMARNOCK
KA1 1BY
01563 576000

EAST DUNBARTONSHIRE COUNCIL
Family Based Care Team
2–4 West High Street
Kirkintilloch
GLASGOW
G66 1AD
0141 7759000
familybasedcare@eastdunbarton.gov.uk

EAST LOTHIAN COUNCIL
Resource Team (Fostering)
Sinclair McGill Building
Lodge Street
HADDINGTON
EH41 3DX
01620 827643

EAST RENFREWSHIRE COUNCIL
Fostering and Adoption Team
Lygates House
224 Ayr Road
NEWTON MEARNS
G77 6DR
0141 577 3367

CITY OF EDINBURGH COUNCIL
Recruitment Team
Springwell House
1 Gorgie Road
EDINBURGH
EH11 2LA
0800 174833
foster.children@edinburgh.gov.uk

**COMHAIRLE NAN EILEAN SIAR
(WESTERN ISLES COUNCIL)**
Fostering Service
Social Work Department
Sandwich Road
STORNOWAY
Isle of Lewis
HS1 2BW
01851 703773

FALKIRK COUNCIL
Adoption and Fostering Team
Brockville
FALKIRK
FK1 5RW
01324 506400

FIFE COUNCIL
Family Placement Services
Social Work Service
16 East Fergus Place
KIRKCALDY
KY1 1XT
01592 412429

GLASGOW CITY COUNCIL
Families for Children
Centenary House
100 Morrison Street
GLASGOW
G5 8LN
0141 420 5555
families.children@glasgow.gov.uk

HIGHLAND COUNCIL
Family Resource Centre
Limetree Avenue
INVERNESS
IV3 5RH
01463 234120

INVERCLYDE COUNCIL
Fostering Services, Children and Families
Social Work and Housing Services
195 Dalrymple Street
GREENOCK
PA15 1UN
01475 714038

MIDLOTHIAN COUNCIL
Family Placement Team
Dalkeith Social Work Centre
11 St Andrews Street
DALKEITH
AH22 1AL
0131 271 3860

MORAY COUNCIL
Fostering and Adoption
Community Services Department

6 Moss Street
ELGIN
Morayshire IV30 1LU
01343 563568

NORTH AYRSHIRE COUNCIL
Family Placement
17–23 Byres Road
KILWINNING
KA13 6JY
01294 559820

NORTH LANARKSHIRE COUNCIL
Adoption and Fostering
Scott House
73/77 Merry Street
MOTHERWELL
ML1 1JE
01698 332676/204
adoptionfamilyplacement@northlan.gov.uk

ORKNEY ISLANDS COUNCIL
Children and Families Team
Council Offices
School Place
KIRKWALL
Orkney KW15 1NY
01856 873535

PERTH AND KINROSS COUNCIL
Fostering and Adoption
Colonsay Resource Centre
37–39 Colonsay Street
North Muirton
PERTH
PH1 3TU
01738 626940

RENFREWSHIRE COUNCIL
Fostering Team
North Buiding
4th Floor
Cotton Street

PAISLEY
PA1 1TZ
0141 842 5158/9

SCOTTISH BORDERS COUNCIL
Family Placement Team
11 Market Street
GALASHIELS
TD1 3AD
01896 757230

SHETLAND ISLANDS COUNCIL
Family Placement
Social Services
92 St Olav's Street
LERWICK
ZE1 0ES
01595 744485

SOUTH AYRSHIRE COUNCIL
Fostering and Adoption Team
Whitlets Area Centre
181 Whitlets Road
AYR
KA8 OJQ
01292 267675

SOUTH LANARKSHIRE COUNCIL
Family Placement Team
1 Leelea Road
HAMILTON
ML3 0XB
01698 454895

STIRLING COUNCIL
Child Care Resource Team (Fostering)
Drummond House
Wellgreen Place
STIRLING
FK8 2EG
01786 471177

WEST DUNBARTONSHIRE COUNCIL
Fostering Service
Department of Social Work
7 Bruce Street
CLYDEBANK
K81 8GI
0141 951 6193

WEST LOTHIAN COUNCIL
Chidren and Families Resource Team
Lomond House
Beveridge Square
LIVINGSTON
EH54 6QF
01506 775959

Voluntary agencies

Voluntary agencies include large children's charities and other organisations which are run on a not-for-profit basis, many of which will have charitable status. They tend to offer high levels of support and training. They will often specialise in foster placements for children with complex needs, and so may prefer to take on more experienced foster carers. Some voluntary agencies run fee-paying schemes for foster carers. For more information on voluntary agencies, see p81.

BARNARDO'S SCOTLAND
Barnardo's runs various fostering projects. We are unable to list them all here. Please contact the address below for further information.
235 Corstorphine Road
EDINBURGH
EH12 7AR
0131 334 9893
www.barnardos.co.uk

JANE MOORE TRUST
Family Placement Service
21 Edinburgh Road
BATHGATE
EH48 1EX
01506 815810
info@thejanemoortrust.org.uk

ST ANDREW'S CHILDREN'S SOCIETY
7 Johns Place
Leith
EDINBURGH
EH6 7EL
0131 454 3370
info@standrews-children.org.uk

ST MARGARET CHILDREN & FAMILY CARE SOCIETY
274 Bath Street
GLASGOW
G2 4JR
0141 332 8371

Independent fostering providers

Independent fostering providers (IFPs) will often be run on a profit-making basis, but some are not and have charitable status. They tend to offer high levels of support and training. They will often specialise in foster placements for children with complex needs, and so may prefer to take on more experienced foster carers. Many independent agencies run fee-paying schemes, and may employ foster carers in the same way as any other business. For more information on IFPs, see p81.

ABERLOUR CHILD CARE TRUST
36 Park Terrace
STIRLING
FK8 2JR
01786 450335
enquiries@aberlour.org.uk

CAROLINA HOUSE TRUST
23 Roseangle
DUNDEE
DD1 4LS
01382 202029
reception@carolina.org.uk

FOSTER CARE ASSOCIATES SCOTLAND
26 Newton Place
GLASGOW
G3 7PY
0141 331 4120
0800 085 2225
www.fostercareassociates.co.uk
contactus@thefca.co.uk

KIBBLE EDUCATION & CARE CENTRE
Intensive Fostering Service
Unit 11
Greenhill Business Park
Greenhill Road
PAISLEY
PA3 1QT
0141 842 3330

Cymru/Wales

Local authorities

Local authorities usually want to place children close to their own families, so tend to prefer applications from people within their area. They will be placing children with a wide range of needs, and so are likely to take on both experienced and less experienced foster carers. For more information on local authorities, see p80.

ISLE OF ANGLESEY COUNTY COUNCIL
Child Placement Team
Housing & Social Services
Council Offices
Llangefni
ANGLESEY
LL77 7TW
01248 752772
maethu-fostering@smartgroups.com

BLAENAU GWENT COUNTY BOROUGH COUNCIL
Fostering and Adoption Team
7 Bridge Street
EBBW VALE
NP23 6EY
01495 355794

BRIDGEND COUNTY BOROUGH COUNCIL
Family Placement Team
Sunnyside
BRIDGEND
CF31 4AR
01656 642349
familyplacement@bridgend.gov.uk

CAERPHILLY COUNTY BOROUGH COUNCIL
Fostering and Adoption
Avenue House
2 King Edward Avenue

CAERPHILLY
CF83 IHE
0800 587 5664

CARDIFF COUNTY COUNCIL
Fostering Team
Children's Services
Greenway Road
Trowbridge
CARDIFF
CF3 1QF
029 2087 2087

CARMARTHENSHIRE COUNTY COUNCIL
Family Placement Team
3rd Floor
Ty Elwyn
LLANELLI
SA15 3AP
01554 742262
socialcare@carmarthenshire.gov.uk

CEREDIGION COUNTY COUNCIL
Contact Centre
Looked After Children and Family Placement Service
Social Services
Minaeron Vicarage Hall
ABERAERON
SA46 ODY
01545 574000
contact-socservs@ceredigion.gov.uk

CONWY COUNTY BOROUGH COUNCIL
The Family Placement Team
Social Services
Civic Annexe
Abergele Road
COLWYN BAY
LL29 8AR
01492 514871

DENBIGHSHIRE COUNTY COUNCIL
Family Placement Liaison Officer
Children's Resource Centre
Cefndy Road
RHYL
LL18 2HG
01824 712200

FLINTSHIRE COUNTY COUNCIL
Family Placement
County Offices
Connah's Quay
DEESIDE
CH5 4HB
01352 701000
fostering@flintshire.gov.uk

GWYNEDD COUNCIL
Family Placement Team
Neuadd Y Dref
BANGOR
LL57 2RE
01286 679810

**MERTHYR TYDFIL BOROUGH
COUNCIL**
Family Placement
Taf Fechan Building
Castle Street
MERTHYR TYDFIL
CF47 8BG
01685 724580

**MONMOUTHSHIRE COUNTY
COUNCIL**
Resource Team
Newbridge House
Baker Street
ABERGAVENNY
NP7 5HU
01873 735900

**NEATH PORT TALBOT COUNTY
BOROUGH COUNCIL**
Community Placement
The Laurels
87 Lewis Road
NEATH
SA11 1DJ
01639 765400

NEWPORT CITY COUNCIL
Fostering Team
The Corn Exchange
High Street
NEWPORT
NP20 1RN
01633 235425
fosteringandadoption@newport.gov.uk

**PEMBROKESHIRE SOCIAL CARE AND
HOUSING DIRECTORATE**
Family Placement Team
The Elms
Golden Hill
PEMBROKE
SA71 4QB
01646 683747

POWYS COUNTY COUNCIL
Family Placement Team
Watton Mount Annexe
The Watton
BRECON
LD3 7DF
01874 624298

RHONDDA CYNON TAFF COUNTY BOROUGH COUNCIL
Looked After Children Service
Lanelay Terrace
Maesycoed
PONTYPRIDD
CF37 1ER
01443 490710

SWANSEA COUNTY COUNCIL
Foster Swansea
Cockett House
Cockett Road
Cockett
SWANSEA
SA2 0FJ
01792 522900
www.fosterswansea.org

TORFAEN COUNTY BOROUGH COUNCIL
Family Placement Team
County Hall

CWMBRAN
NP44 2WN
01633 648540

VALE OF GLAMORGAN COUNCIL
Fostering Team
3rd Floor
Haydock House
1 Holton Road
BARRY
CF63 4HA
01446 725288
fostercare@valeofglamorgan.gov.uk

WREXHAM COUNTY BOROUGH COUNCIL
Family Placement Team
Kelso House (rear)
13 Grosvenor Road
WREXHAM
LL11 1DB
0800 783 0618
fostering@wrexham.gov.uk

Voluntary agencies

Voluntary agencies include large children's charities and other organisations which are run on a not-for-profit basis, many of which will have charitable status. They tend to offer high levels of support and training. They will often specialise in foster placements for children with complex needs, and so may prefer to take on more experienced foster carers. Some voluntary agencies run fee-paying schemes for foster carers. For more information on voluntary agencies, see p81.

BARNARDO'S CYMRU
Barnardo's runs various fostering projects. We are unable to list them all here. Please contact the address below for further information.

11–15 Columbus Walk
Brigantine Place
Atlantic Wharf
CARDIFF
CF10 4BZ
029 2049 3387
www.barnardos.co.uk

Independent fostering providers

Independent fostering providers (IFPs) will often be run on a profit-making basis, but some are not and have charitable status. They tend to offer high levels of support and training. They will often specialise in foster placements for children with complex needs, and so may prefer to take on more experienced foster carers. Many independent agencies run fee-paying schemes, and may employ foster carers in the same way as any other business. For more information on IFPs, see p81.

FOSTER CARE ASSOCIATES CYMRU (SOUTH)
57 Walter Road
SWANSEA
SA1 5PZ
01792 644442
0800 085 2225
www.fostercareassociates.co.uk
contactus@thefca.co.uk

FOSTER CARE ASSOCIATES CYMRU (NORTH)
3 Wynnslay Road
COLWYN BAY

LL29 8NB
0800 085 2225
www.fostercareassociates.co.uk
contactus@thefca.co.uk

PATHWAY CARE LIMITED
Unit 10
Village Way
Tongwynlais
CARDIFF
CF15 7NE
029 2081 1173
www.pathwaycare.com

Useful organisations

British Association for Adoption & Fostering (BAAF)

BAAF is a registered charity and professional association for all those working in the child care field. BAAF's work includes: giving advice and information to members of the public on aspects of adoption, fostering and child care issues; publishing a wide range of books, training packs and leaflets as well as a quarterly journal on adoption, fostering and child care issues; providing training and consultancy services to social workers and other professionals to help them improve the quality of medical, legal and social work services to children and families; responding to consultative documents on changes in legislation and regulations affecting children in or at risk of coming into care; and helping to find new families for children through *Be My Parent*.

More information about BAAF can be obtained from our offices listed below.

Head Office
Skyline House
200 Union Street
London SE1 0LX
Tel: 020 7593 2000
Email: mail@baaf.org.uk
www.baaf.org.uk

Be My Parent
Address as Head Office
Tel: 020 7593 2060/1/2

BAAF England

Central and Northern Region
Grove Villa, 82 Cardigan Road
Headingley
Leeds LS6 3BJ
Tel: 0113 274 4797
Email: leeds@baaf.org.uk

and at:
Dolphin House
54 Coventry Road
Birmingham B10 0RX
Tel: 0121 753 2001
Email: midlands@baaf.org.uk

and at:
MEA House
Ellison Place
Newcastle-upon-Tyne NE1 8XS
Tel: 0191 261 6600
Email: newcastle@baaf.org.uk

Southern Region
Skyline House
200 Union Street
London SE1 0LX
Tel: 020 7593 2041/2
Email: southern@baaf.org.uk

BAAF Cymru
7 Cleeve House
Lambourne Crescent
Cardiff CF14 5GP
Tel: 029 2076 1155
Email: cymru@baaf.org.uk

and at
Suite C, 1st Floor
Darkgate, 3 Red Street
Carmarthen SA31 1QL
Tel: 01267 221000
Email: carmarthen@baaf.org.uk

and at
19 Bedford Street
Rhyl
Denbighshire LL18 1SY
Tel: 01745 336336
Email: rhyl@baaf.org.uk

BAAF Scotland
40 Shandwick Place
Edinburgh EH2 4RT
Tel: 0131 220 4749
Email: scotland@baaf.org.uk

| **Fostering Network**

The Fostering Network is a membership organisation for everyone involved in fostering. It campaigns for higher standards of care for fostered children and young people, and gives support to fostering services and foster carers.

The Fostering Network provides a 24-hour legal advice service, runs training courses, and publishes a quarterly magazine, *Foster Care*, and a range of books for foster carers, social workers and other professionals.

Head Office
87 Blackfriars Road
London SE1 8HA
Tel: 020 7620 6400
www.fostering.net

The Fostering Network in Scotland
2nd Floor Ingram House
227 Ingram Street
Glasgow G1 1DA
Tel: 0141 204 1400

The Fostering Network in Northern Ireland
216 Belmont Road
Belfast BT4 2AT
Tel: 02890 673 441

The Fostering Network in Wales
Suite 11, 2nd Floor
Bay Chambers
West Bute Street
Cardiff Bay CF10 5BB
Tel: 02920 440 940

| **Other useful organisations**

Contact a Family

Provides support, advice and information for carers of children with disabilities, and helps to put families in touch with each other.

209–211 City Road
London EC1V 1JN
Tel: 020 7608 8700
Helpline: 0808 808 3555

National Council of Voluntary Child Care Organisations

Offers information, training and advice to voluntary child care organisations. Individual supporters can subscribe to their monthly news bulletin and quarterly journal.

Unit 4, Pride Court
80–82 White Lion Street
London N1 9PF
Tel: 020 7833 3319

NCH

Works to improve the lives of vulnerable children by offering a range of services, including residential, foster care and adoption services, leaving care services and short break projects. Produces a variety of leaflets and information.

NCH England
85 Highbury Park
London N5 1UD
Tel: 020 7704 7000

NCH Cymru
St David's Court
68a Cowbridge Road East
Cardiff
CF11 9DN
Tel: 029 2022 2127

NCH Scotland
17 Newton Place
Glasgow
G3 7PY
Tel: 0141 332 4041

The Who Cares? Trust

Works to improve public care for children and young people who are separated from their families and living in residential or foster care.

Head Office
Kemp House
152–160 City Road
London EC1V 2NP
Tel: 020 7251 3117

Who Cares? Scotland

Committed to improving the standard of life for all looked after children and young people in Scotland. The organisation also works to raise awareness of the problems affecting young people who are or have been looked after.

Who Cares? Scotland
Head Office
Oswald Chambers
5 Oswald Street
Glasgow
G1 4QR
Tel: 0141 226 4441

Children in Scotland

The national agency for voluntary,
statutory and professional organisations
and individuals working with children
and their families in Scotland. They
provide training, publications and the
monthly magazine, *Children in
Scotland*.

Princes House
5 Shandwick Place
Edinburgh
EH12 4RG
Tel: 0131 228 8484

Useful publications

| BOOKS FOR ADULTS

**The books listed below are available from BAAF. Please visit
www.baaf.org.uk or contact 020 7593 2072 for more details.**

Parenting

**Caroline Archer, *First Steps in Parenting the Child who Hurts*, Jessica Kingsley
Publishers, 1999**

**Caroline Archer, *Next Steps in Parenting the Child who Hurts*, Jessica Kingsley
Publishers, 1999**
These books offer practical, sensitive guidance through the areas of separation, loss
and trauma in early childhood, and into adolescence. The effects of early emotional
trauma are explained, and the author reviews specific sensitive situations that
commonly arise.

Brian Cairns, *Fostering Attachments*, BAAF, 2004
This compelling book describes the unusual model of family group care undertaken
by Brian and Kate Cairns, whose three birth children and 12 foster children lived
together in their family home. Brian describes the benefits of family group
membership in aiding learning and recovery for children who have had difficult
pasts.

Kate Cairns, *Attachment, Trauma and Resilience*, BAAF, 2002
Draws on Kate's personal experiences with three birth children and 12 fostered
children to describe family life with children who have experienced attachment
difficulties, loss and trauma, and suggests what can be done to promote recovery
and develop resilience.

Vera Fahlberg, *A Child's Journey through Placement*, BAAF, 1995, reprinted 2004
Invaluable for all those involved in childcare, this book contains the theoretical
knowledge base and skills necessary for understanding and working with children
who are separated from their families. Comprehensive sections on attachment,
separation and child development are included, all illustrated with case studies.

**Stephen Hicks and Janet McDermott (eds), *Lesbian and Gay Fostering and
Adoption*, Jessica Kingsley Publishers, 1998**
This immensely readable book will be of great encouragement to lesbians or gay
men considering fostering or adoption. It tells openly and honestly how it is,

without resorting to jargon or becoming weighted down with politics.

Claudia Jewett, *Helping Children cope with Separation and Loss*, **BAAF/Batsford, 1995**
Using case histories and simple dialogues, this book details a range of simple techniques that adults can use to help children through their experiences of grief and loss.

Catherine Macaskill, *Adopting or Fostering a Sexually Abused Child*, **BAAF/Batsford, 1991**
This book describes the findings of a 1989 research project covering 80 placements of abused children. It discusses the implications for all involved, discussing how to help children talk through their experiences, and the impact on other children in the family.

Foster care studies

Gillian Schofield, Mary Beek and Kay Sargent with June Thoburn, *Growing up in Foster Care*, **BAAF, 2000**
For a significant group of children, long-term foster care is their best chance of a secure family life. This research study follows 58 children, their foster carers, birth parents and childcare workers, looking at the impact of abuse, neglect and separation on the children's behaviour.

Mary Beek and Gillian Schofield, *Providing a Secure Base in Long-term Foster Care*, **BAAF, 2004**
This study records progress over three years of the group of children first met in *Growing up in Foster Care*, and describes how many of the children were beginning to relinquish some of their more troubled behaviours. First-hand accounts add depth and immediacy to the book.

Gillian Schofield, *Part of the Family: Pathways through foster care*, **BAAF, 2002**
Based on the stories of 40 young adults who were fostered long-term, the author describes the varied routes that children can take through foster care, looking at what made some experiences successful and others less so.

Moira Walker, Malcolm Hill and John Triseliotis, *Testing the Limits of Foster Care*, **BAAF, 2002**
This study looks at the pioneering Community Alternative Placement Scheme (CAPS), set up by NCH Action for Children in Scotland, highlighting how high-quality foster care can allow many children from secure care to remain in the community.

Useful guides

Kate Cairns and Chris Stanway, *Learn the Child*, BAAF, 2004
A resource pack (containing a book and CD-ROM with a Powerpoint presentation) which looks at how foster carers, teachers and social workers can help looked after children to gain full benefit from their lives at school.

Robbie Gilligan, *Promoting Resilience*, BAAF, 2001
This pioneering book applies the concept of resilience to work with children in residential and foster care. Packed with practical ideas on how to improve the quality of life for children in care using relationship networks in their family, school and leisure activities.

Rena Phillips (ed), *Children Exposed to Parental Substance Misuse*, BAAF, 2004
This anthology considers the psychological, social and behavioural impact on children exposed to parental substance misuse. Medical experts provide useful information on the effects of certain drugs and alcohol, and social work practitioners consider how best children can be helped.

Tony Ryan and Rodger Walker, *Life Story Work*, BAAF, 1999
This popular and practical guide is essential reading for anyone involved in life story work with children. Accessibly presented and attractively illustrated.

Advice Note, *Private Fostering*, BAAF, 1998
Aimed at those considering private fostering in England and Wales, this leaflet explains what it involves and provides guidance.

The two books listed below are available from Fostering Network. Please visit www.fostering.net or contact 0845 4589910 for more details.

***All about Fostering*, Fostering Network**
Presented in a highly accessible, magazine-style format, this introductory guide answers the common questions people have when considering fostering. Personal experiences and opinions of existing foster carers, social workers and young people are included.

***Becoming a Foster Carer*, Fostering Network**
An essential guide for people going through the assessment process to become foster carers, which sets out what happens during the stages of assessment.

| **BOOKS FOR CHILDREN**

The books listed below are available from BAAF. Please visit www.baaf.org.uk or contact 020 7593 2072 for more details.

Bruce's Multimedia Story, **CD-ROM, Information Plus, 1998**
Bruce's Multimedia Story raises issues about identity and change, capitalising on children's natural interest in computer-based activities. Animation, sound effects and music make the whole experience more productive for worker and child. Runs under Windows 3.1, Windows 95 or on Macintosh.

Hedi Argent and Mary Lane, *What Happens in Court?*, BAAF, 2003
A user-friendly guide to help children understand the role a court might have in their lives. Easily understandable and brightly illustrated.

Sheila Byrne and Leigh Chambers, *Feeling Safe*, BAAF, 1998
Tina has to go into foster care following abuse in the home.

Sheila Byrne and Leigh Chambers, *Waiting for the Right Home*, BAAF, 2001
Daniel is in short-term foster care, waiting to go home.

Jean Camis, *My Life and Me*, BAAF, 2001
This colourful and comprehensive life story book will help children living apart from their families develop and record memories of their past. Written by a social worker with extensive experience of direct work with children, *My Life and Me* is supplied with practice guidelines.

Jean Camis, *We are Fostering*, BAAF, 2003
Designed along similar lines to *My Life and Me*, this colourful and durable workbook will help birth children to know their history and role in the family, and prepare them to welcome foster brothers and sisters into their homes and lives.

Angela Lidster, *Chester and Daisy Move on*, BAAF, 1999
This popular and engaging picture book is for use with children aged 4–10 who are moving on to adoption, to help them explore feelings about their past and their moves, and to help carers identify these issues from the child's perspective.

Barbara Orritt, *Dennis Duckling*, The Children's Society, 1999
Dennis, an appealing little duckling, has to leave his family as they can no longer look after him. He goes to live on a new pond where he begins to make new friends and is cared for by grown-up ducks. Suitable for use with children aged 4–8.

Shaila Shah, *Fostering: What it is and what it means*, BAAF, 2003
This is a short, brightly illustrated guide to fostering for children and young people,

covering the different types of fostering, how children come to be fostered, parents, contact and many other questions. Designed to be worked through with a child before and during foster care.

The books listed below are available from Amazon. Please visit www.amazon.co.uk for more details.

Sharon Creech, *Ruby Holler*, Bloomsbury, 2003
Dallas and Florida live in the Boxton Creek Home, and have a reputation for rule-breaking and being "difficult to place". But the unconventional elderly couple who offer them a foster placement have a patient and unobtrusive approach to parenting which turns out to be just right. Suitable for children aged 10 and upwards.

Martina Selway, *So Many Babies*, Red Fox, 2003
Mrs Badger doesn't know what to do with her extra rooms until she reads that there are 'so many babies' who need her care. She starts with just one but ends up with so many children that she needs to build an extension. Told in rhyme and with the counting elements adding an additional bonus, this book is helpful for young children who are fostered.

Jacqueline Wilson, *The Story of Tracy Beaker*, Yearling Books, 1992
Tracy is ten years old. She lives in a Children's Home but would like a real home one day. Written as Tracy's diary, this is a lively, humorous book which reveals a lot of what goes on in the minds of children separated from their parents. Winner of several awards and adapted for television.

Jacqueline Wilson, *The Dare Game*, Yearling Books, 2001
The sequel to *The Story of Tracy Beaker*. Tracy is now settled in the home of her foster carer, Cam. Tracy had imagined everything would be perfect but finds this is not the case. When playing truant from school, she meets two boys also dealing with problems in their lives.

Jacqueline Wilson, *Dustbin Baby*, Yearling Books, 2002
Fourteen-year-old April was abandoned as a baby in a dustbin, and has since been through a failed adoption, a foster home, a children's home and a special school. But she is now able to find out who really cares about her. A highly readable account of the mixed emotions of an abandoned child, providing children and adults with insights about how it feels to be "in care".

Sample application form

The following sample application form is an example of the sort of form you may have to fill in when first applying to be a foster carer. It has been reproduced with the kind permission of Medway Council.

e-form | **Fostering Application** | *Medway*

Fostering application initial information form:

Marital status:
Single ○   Married ○   Partnership ○   **foStering**

Your name(s):
Applicant 1:

Surname [_____]

Forename(s) [_____]

Title [____] Other [_____]

Date of birth [_____]

Applicant 2:

Surname [_____]

Forename(s) [_____]

Title [____] Other [_____]

Date of birth [_____]

Contact details:

Daytime phone [_____]

Evening phone [_____]

Mobile phone [_____]

Email [_____]

---

e-form   **Fostering Application**   *Medway*

Your address:

Surname

Forename(s)

Title

Flat number

House number   House name

Street

Locality

Town

County

Postcode

Select an address:

Fostering Application *Medway*

Previous address(s) (In the past 5 years):

Marriage/partnership details:

Date of marriage

Place of marriage

Length of partnership [ ] years

Previous marriages:

Applicant 1:

Have you been married before? Yes ○ No ○

How many times? [ ]

Applicant 2:

Have you been married before? Yes ○ No ○

How many times? [ ]

Details about the applicant(s) and their household (family members):

Details about the applicant(s) and their household (non-family members):

e-form   **Fostering Application**   *Medway*

Accommodation details:

Accommodation type [   ]

Property type [   ]   Other [   ]

How many bedrooms? [   ]

Will foster children have their own bedroom?   Yes ○ No ○

Have any adaptations been made to your home to   Yes ○ No ○
accommodate a child with disability?

Is a garden available?   Yes ○ No ○

Number and type of
pets in home.   [   ]

Is there a car available during the day?   Yes ○ No ○

Health details:

Do you have any health problems?   Yes ○ No ○

Please state the nature of the
problem(s) and whether it is a   [   ]
long term problem.

Are you registered as a person with a disability?   Yes ○ No ○

Please state the nature of the
disability.   [   ]

Do you smoke?

Applicant 1: Yes ○ No ○

Applicant 2: Yes ○ No ○

e-form   **Fostering Application**   *Medway*

Previous fostering:

Have you made a previous application to become a foster carer?   Yes ○ No ○

Please state details, when, to whom and the outcome of the application.

Have you ever fostered privately or for another agency/voluntary organisation?   Yes ○ No ○

Please state details.

Have you had in your care any child, not being related to you, who has been removed from your care by a court order?   Yes ○ No ○

Have you been prohibited from keeping any child who is not related to you, under the Children Act 1989, The Foster Placement (Children) Regulations 1991 or any Act of Parliament?   Yes ○ No ○

Have you or any other person in your household been convicted of any offence relating to children?   Yes ○ No ○

Please state details.

Details of fostering:

Duration of care:

Short term care ○   Long term/permanency ○

Number of children:

Female [   ]

Male [   ]

Either [   ]

Siblings:

We are interested in looking after [   ]

Childrens age group:

0 - 2 ☐   3 - 5 ☐   6 - 10 ☐   11 - 13 ☐   14 - 16 ☐   16 + ☐

Is this application in relation to a specific child?   Yes ○ No ○

Completing this section does not commit you to the categories you have ticked.

e-form **Fostering Application**   *Medway*

Specific child:

Surname

Forename(s)

Date of birth

Address of child:

Flat number

House number   House name

Street

Locality

Town

County

Postcode

Relationship:

Please state your relationship
to the child.

Could you foster a child who (please tick all the boxes that apply):

is from a different ethnic/religious background from yourself?   ☐

is a teenager remanded to the care of the local authority?   ☐

has learning difficulties and is attending a special school?   ☐

has a physical disability?   ☐

has severe multiple disabilities?   ☐

has emotional problems?   ☐

has hearing difficulties?   ☐

has been physically and/or sexually abused and/or neglected?   ☐

is a teenager needing preparation for independent living?   ☐

e-_form_   **Fostering Application**   _Medway_

Have you any experience or skills you feel would be helpful in fostering? (please specify)

Is there any information that you would like that is not on the web pages?
Please feel free to call us or ask a question here.

I/we understand that by submitting this information it is acknowledged that it is to the best of my/our knowledge true.

I/we have no objection to the Health and Community Services Directorate making enquiries about me/us.

I/we recognise that the Health and Community Services Directorate has the right to refuse my/our application and any information disclosed to them about me/us from a third party may not be shared with me/us.

foStering

Application Date: 04/05/2004